BRAINSTORMING

The Practical Guide to Mastering Creative

(Instructions to Make Your Brainstorming
Sessions More Profitable)

Homer Hargrave

Published By Homer Hargrave

Homer Hargrave

Brainstorming: The Practical Guide to Mastering Creative (Instructions to Make Your Brainstorming Sessions More Profitable)

ISBN 978-1-77485-424-2

Legal & Disclaimer

The information contained in this book is not designed to replace or take the place of any form of medicine or professional medical advice. The information in this book has been provided for educational and entertainment purposes only.

The information contained in this book has been compiled from sources deemed reliable, and it is accurate to the best of the Author's knowledge; however, the Author cannot guarantee its accuracy and validity and cannot be held liable for any errors or omissions. Changes are periodically made to this book. You must consult your doctor or get professional medical advice before using any of the suggested remedies, techniques, or information in this book.

TABLE OF CONTENTS

Introduction

Have you ever attempted to come up with a novel cocktail recipe as well as a creative idea for a kid's birthday celebration, a fresh method to arrange the furniture in your room, or deciding on the perfect gift to send off your colleague? It's not an easy task especially when you are trying to come up with something unique or unique, as if we often fall into the trap of making variants of the exact same idea often.

Imagine pouring water on a flat soil surface. The pressure of the water's impact on the soil causes grooves and dents which let the water disperse. Imagine spreading it out several times until the water settles down into the specific path. It doesn't make new grooves or dents, but instead is focused on the tracks in place to determine its route. This is the way that most people approach the idea generation process using their experiences in the past to discover innovative solutions. Henry Ford, the legendary American businessman and creator of Ford Motor, once said, "If I had asked people what they wanted they would have answered more horses!" Everyone were aware that they wanted to travel faster, but many (not all) (not Henry Ford!) were unable to think outside their mental boundaries.

Habits are the same as thinking patterns. They are formed over time and once they are established in place, it's hard to alter them. While forming specific patterns of thinking (i.e. methods to solve issues) can save us a good amount of mental energy carrying out our day-to-day tasks, they're generally not a good way to come up with new and innovative concepts.

Chapter 1: The Reasons For Brainstorming?

At some point or another chances are you've participated in brainstorming sessions. This is a task that everyone believes they can do however, very few do it very well. The outcome of your brainstorming session being an enjoyable and fruitful experience or boring and ineffective is contingent on how it's organized and controlled.

Just a bit of planning can boost the value of every brainstorming session you conduct...and an idea-gathering session which isn't a success is costly. A poorly-run brainstorming session can are prone to low quality of ideas. It can lead to the implementation of poor ideas or failing to make any adjustments. These outcomes demoralize and frustrate those anyone who took part in the brainstorming sessions. Naturally, this is your opposite goal from what wanted to accomplish.

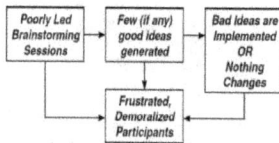

The price of poorly-planned and executed brainstorming sessions is as follows:

* Cost of man-hours to gather a group of people to a common place

•Costs associated with the implementation of poor ideas that were generated during the brainstorming session

OR - OR -

*Costs related to not implementing alternatives or best practices which is the cost of continuing to "business as normal"

*Cost of having frustrated and demoralized

participants/employees/members/custom ers

Cost of loss of management credibility

*Cost of losing future participation for the people that have lost faith in the process , and/or your management

It is possible to avoid these costs by planning and implementing efficient brainstorming sessions. This book offers guidelines and suggestions on how to run brainstorming sessions that draw out the best and most innovative ideas from everyone.

Brainstorming is the act of the process of allowing ideas to flow without evaluation of their merit, rationality or cost effectiveness. It is also a method of determining if they are achievable or any other aspect. This is crucial. If negative feedback is introduced into discussion, it's interpreted as criticism, and people are more cautious in speaking about ideas that pop into their the mind. In most cases, it's the most absurd thought that ignites an idea that eventually gets explored.

Based on the method described above, it is possible to conclude the existence of two fundamental guidelines for brainstorming:

* There is no thing as a bad idea.

No negative or critical feedback is permitted during the brainstorming sessions.

Have you ever observed an ice crack? It starts slowly , with just only one crack, but accelerates as cracks form around the crack. Some cracks are large while others are smaller however, every time a crack is created the cause for cracks to develop. In time, the frequency of cracks decreases. If you only put some tension on the frozen ice the process will begin again.

Brainstorming is like cracking ice.

When an idea is proposed and a variety of ideas are derived from it. Certain ideas appear in full form - ideas that are able to enter your brain. Others begin with a small fissure slowly moving towards the surface of your brain. Once they are at the top of your list and you speak about them, others are closely following closely. Then, the new ideas start to emerge slower or cease altogether. Sometimes, a slight pressure from an external stimulant can trigger the process over.

This book will assist you to make the ice melt and will teach you ways of applying a bit of pressure when ideas begin to flow more slowly. Before we dive deep into brainstorming, let's take a look at some recent research that indicates that brainstorming is an exercise that is not conducive to creativity.

New Research in Brainstorming

Since the very first research into brainstorming in 1958, a variety of studies have proven that group brainstorming produces less ideas than the same amount of people working independently. Furthermore, the ideas that were generated were feasible to implement. In the end, it appears that when working in a group everyone thought about the issue more deeply.

Further studies have revealed that altering one of the Osborn's fundamental rules of brainstorming, which is no criticism of ideas encouraged more imaginative thinking and practical thinking. A study discovered that the introduction of bad concepts - that is, concepts that were not practical or did not address the issue while allowing the an evaluation or discussion of the ideas boosted creativity by participants.

My experience has shown that brainstorming can be a powerful method for coming up with creative ideas in a group However, the Osborn model could be tweaked to achieve the best outcomes. While studies have proven the greater number of ideas can be created by individuals working on their own to solve a challenge however, these studies typically examined the results of a group people brainstorming together with the same amount of people working on ideas independently in the same circumstances as the group, i.e free of distractions by distractions and for the same duration. The issue with this research is that the disciplined brainstorming that is required in research isn't possible in the current society of "always another deadline to be met or a phone call to be answered or a task to work on."

One of the benefits of gathering a group is the control of the surroundings and having a few individuals who are focused on the topic to be discussed.

Furthermore, it's not typical for managers to assign the same issue to several individuals and then have them come back with as many suggestions as is possible.

Another benefit of having an entire group closer is how many participants are involved in finding solutions or coming up with the next brilliant idea.

Understanding the findings of recent research can help us adjust our approach to brainstorming and the guidelines to gain the maximum value from the process. Another benefits of brainstorming is that it can be extremely efficient in forming and energizing teams to work in a cohesive manner. If well-planned, a properly executed brainstorming session can boost the team's interaction and also each participant's feel a sense of ownership for the idea or solution that is to be implemented.

Chapter 2: Preparing For Creativity

The Identification of Your Participants and Moderators

While spontaneous brainstorming sessions are often productive however, spending a bit of time the process will result in a wider range of ideas that are created from the participants. Before we talk about how to plan for this brainstorming exercise, lets take a look at the methods to choose participants and choose the moderator.

Go it alone or finding the Group

As I mentioned earlier the research on brainstorming has proven that there are more ideas created by people working on their own instead of working as an organization. However, I do prefer group brainstorming due to the chain reactions of ideas that result. The group brainstorming process brings diverse experiences of several individuals to work on an issue or topic.

There are many who don't have the luxury of a group, however. We'll discuss the process of brainstorming in a group. You'll get ways to brainstorm on your own in Chapter 4.

Identifying Your Brainstorming Group

In determining your brainstorming group, you must the decision of how many people to include as well as who they should be. This article will address both of these issues and Appendix 1 includes a checklist to make use of when determining the group you're brainstorming with.

Keep the group to a small size. It is best to form an enclave of between three and six people. If you're a group of more than six persons it is possible to break them into two groups. Each group is able to brainstorm about the same subject or various aspects of the topic. The idea of brainstorming with a group of more than six participants is usually not productive. One of two things are likely to occur:

The group is a mess and the mood quickly degrades into a gathering at which there is nothing worthwhile accomplished. The swarm of partying group of brainstormers, they are unable to bring new ideas on the table.

* Some people have ideas to come up with however those who do not be thinking as fast as the others, and instead start to check their email or text messages. They also look at ceiling tiles. Inviting these people into the conversation while others are advancing with new ideas feels as if they're being punished, which isn't a good way to promote fresh ideas.

Keep your group small and you'll see that interaction between participants is more vibrant and healthy.

Various backgrounds bring different experiences. It is important to form groups of people who have diverse backgrounds, perspectives and personality. Five people from five diverse backgrounds, experiences and perspectives are likely produce more thoughts and have a greater range of thoughts than those who have similar experiences and backgrounds. If Joe for example who's been running a non-profit organization is presented with the idea of Alice who's spent two years working as a sales rep at an innovative company at first, he may think it's a bit crazy. When he's turned the idea around in his head a bit however, he's more likely to suggest a similar idea from a different angle. Jerry is the customer of a small tools firm, will be able to hear the two ideas and come up with a third perspective on the idea. And the list goes on. You'll get the picture.

Different personalities provide different ideas. In the same way, individuals with different personality types approach situations and think about information differently. For instance, administrators tend to think about goal setting. Goal setting might be irrelevant for engineers who think about problem solving. Artists think visually while scientists think conceptually. The act of bringing different kinds of people together in an idea-sharing session could lead to ideas that are out of the ordinary.

How well the participants get to know each other can affect the success of your project. Along with selecting participants from different backgrounds and with different personalities The right mixture of participants can affect the results you achieve. A study showed that the lowest results came during brainstorming sessions if:

* All of the participants knew each other as well.

* All participants did not have enough acquaintances to.

If all of the participants had been working together for some time it led to the absence of ideas that were fresh. If the participants didn't know one the other well enough, they felt not comfortable taking the risk of offering out-of-the-box ideas. The most effective group is composed mainly of people who are familiar with each other well enough to be able to suggest unconventional ideas to two or three others who aren't familiar with the group and , therefore, provide fresh perspectives.

Your participants must share enough similarities to be a good decision to contribute ideas to the topic being discussed and they may share an concern about the topic or are employed by the same company or are part of the same company. This is your first step.

Begin to create your team by introducing diversity in the backgrounds and personalities Then, shake the group to make it more interesting by adding a person who the team members do not know as well. This should result in the perfect group for getting to know each other well and coming up new and innovative ideas.

If you frequently plan brainstorming sessions, make sure that you do not invite identical group of people to every session no matter if the topic is identical or distinct. Variate the group members to achieve the most effective outcomes.

If your group is found to having members who don't have a good relationship or meet regularly You should think about having a warm-up brainstorming session before the start of each meeting. Check out Preparing the Presentation on the next page for more information on this.

Picking a Moderator

The moderator of the brainstorming session is a crucial role. The moderator must plan for the meeting, introduce the subject for discussion to participants, and then moderate when ideas start to flow and close the session to the session when the session is over. The moderator's duties are discussed in greater detail throughout this section. Understanding these responsibilities is essential in deciding on the moderator.

Making preparations to attend the Brainstorming Session

Once the moderator has been chosen, the actual preparation of the session commences. It is their duty to finish each of the tasks listed below:

* Choose the best method or approach for brainstorming.
* Create the presentation
* Preparing the venue
* Gather the necessary supplies
* Invite members of the group
* Choose an audio recorder
* Plan for what will happen following the brainstorming session

Naturally, the moderator needs to take some time in preparing for the meeting. Every one of those tasks will be detailed in the next paragraphs.

A checklist for Moderators Responsibilities has been provided to aid you in tracking your preparation.

Choosing an Approach or a Technique

Are you using the well-tested method or will you employ some modifications? Study Chapter 3 to understand the basics of brainstorming and to learn alternative methods. These alternatives to the standard method can add a touch of flavor to your brainstorming session and can be useful with groups who are incredibly shy or for groups that regularly brainstorm together.

The preparation of the presentation

Presenting the subject for the entire group in a manner that unleash the full creativity of each participant is essential. The moderator must take into consideration the members of the group brainstorming as they prepare the initial presentation. Are the members of the group abstract or concrete thinkers? Are they process or goal focused? The goal is to explain the subject in a way that participants fully comprehend the concept while inducing them to utilize their experiences, knowledge opinions, and interactions with each other to let their imaginations run wild.

It is at this period that the moderator can put the group at relaxed. If it is individuals who have not worked together before, the moderator needs to plan a warm-up or practice brainstorming session in the initial few minutes. In this rehearsal the group could brainstorm about an absurd topic. It can bring people together and help get participants comfortable with the procedure.

Effective presentations will accomplish these things:

* Include at least two elements:

The presentation will focus on the issue or issue that is being discussed.

Guidelines for effective brainstorming. (See Annexe 1 for the guidelines you can copy and distribute for participants.)

* Warm-up or practice session If suitable.

* Keep it short. Do not bore your brainstorming group and invite them to think creatively. Keep your presentation brief in the presentation of the topic as well as the guidelines for brainstorming.

After all the work is done, you must be able present your brainstorming topic in just one or two sentences.

* Define the issue or issue to be brainstormed correctly. Consider the goal of the brainstorming session prior to defining the subject. It isn't a good idea to waste time and money on an issue that isn't relevant.

Restate the subject maybe in a different manner. You must ensure everybody is in the same boat before getting to work.

* Allow enough time for questions in order to ensure everyone understands the subject being discussed.

* Make sure that the group members are comfortable with the procedure and each other. Moderators should develop an exercise to the group to work in case the group isn't at ease with each other. Here are some suggestions:

* You're in a small gathering at the home of a friend and discover a cockroach on your salad. What do you do?

* Let's brainstorm chapter titles to an upcoming book that I'm writing brainstorming.

* How do we transform the world, without paying greater than $50?

What is the best way for your local team of sports do to increase ticket sales?

As part of creating the presentation the moderator needs to come up with ideas and questions to facilitate the development of ideas:

Make a list of questions could be used to kick off the discussion following the presentation. The questions should be related to the subject, but they should be approached in a different manner or from a different angle to spark the imagination of all participants.

Create five or six questions could be used to encourage imagination during brainstorming sessions. Do not dump all the questions onto the group all at once, but add them gradually to keep the discussion lively. The questions could suggest an alternative perspective to look at the subject from or the challenge that is inherent to the subject.

As an example, suppose that the entire family has gathered to discuss summer activities. The moderator should explain the requirements for the activities (such as the amount of time and funds are available) and then be prepared to answer questions like:

* What kind of trips or activities are fun and exciting for you?

* Cold or hot? Dry or wet? Luxury or rustic? What kinds of activities can meet these criteria?

* Quickly! List things you've always wanted for an hour's driving from your home.

* Come up with a few crazy ideas you could bring into the discussion when the creativity wane.

* Let's try parasailing with grandma! (OK it's true that in certain families, it could be considered normal but in my household it's pretty shocking!)

Making the Venue

The location you hold your brainstorming session can be a major factor in its success. It is recommended to hold your brainstorming session in a different location than the normal setting. It's amazing how this affects the circulation of thoughts. If you're hosting meetings for brainstorming in the same room where weekly meetings for staff are held, the attendees enter with an "staff meeting" mentality. What is the typical format for staff meetings? Staff members report on their performance and get new tasks. This kind of attitude isn't ideal for spontaneous brainstorming. Instead, locate a comfy place, and then create a space that is as welcoming as you can. Check out Making Your Brainstorming Sessions More Fun and productive for more ideas.

Invited Group Members to Join

I've already talked about the best way to choose group members to participate in an idea-sharing session. After you have identified your members of your group and picked the venue you can invite everyone. Make sure you require an RSVP in order to invite additional guests if any members cannot attend.

Gathering Materials

Every idea should be documented in a manner that is accessible to all, so you can use a smartboard or chalkboard, poster board size paper, or a projection of a computer on a wall or something similar. If participants can see the ideas they generate in a clear way, they can concentrate and come up with new ideas.

If you've decided to utilize one of the alternative brainstorming methods described in Chapter 3.3, you'll need collect the necessary supplies for the method.

Finally, gather the supplies you will need to make your brainstorming session more enjoyable and productive. Learn How to Make Your Brainstorming Sessions More Fun and productive for more specific suggestions.

Picking a Recorder

The moderator may also wish to choose a recorder that can publish the ideas to the group while they arise. A well-designed recorder will inspire the group however, a bad one can bring the flow of creative ideas to a halt. The recorder should be able to distill ideas into few words and then create them quickly for the group to read. If the process is longer than the time needed for every idea then the group will spend more time looking at the recorder rather than the ideas can bounce around. If the description written isn't capturing the concept well it can affect all concepts that follow it. It also can cause confusion when ideas are analyzed at the end of the meeting.

Preparing for post-brainstorming

What happens after the brainstorming session has ended? This is a crucial issue to be answered before beginning the meeting. Do the participants conduct an analysis of the ideas after the conclusion or at the end of your session? Do you plan to bring members back to further refine some of the ideas? Are you going to work with a different group of people? decide what ideas you want to explore? How will you convey your findings from the meeting to the participants?

It's crucial to decide on these issues before you start your brainstorming session . You should also share them with your group. Your initial presentation to the group brainstorming should contain a brief explanation of what's going to happen next. Don't let the group think whether their efforts were wasted time.

A clear idea of what you will do following the brainstorming session can help you conclude the discussion effectively and effectively communicate with the team members.

Modifying the Brainstorming Session

During the brainstorming sessions, the moderator is responsible for the following duties:

* Discuss the subject with the group.
* Control your flow of thoughts
* Make sure to close the session properly
• Follow up with the participants
* Start the evaluation process for ideas If it is appropriate

Discussion of the Topic

Keep your presentation lively when presenting the idea to your brainstorming team. Be sure to not let questions steer you off the topic during your presentation. Respond to questions that will improve the understanding of the group on the subject; leave others to later discussions.

Define your function as moderator. That is, your job is to bring the group back to their subject when they wander and to remind them of the rules if the system is beginning to fall apart.

Facilitate the brainstorming session.

Once brainstorming has begun the primary responsibility of the moderator is to make sure that the group adheres to rules such as the "no criticizing ideas" rule, and to find the right balance between letting wild ideas flow but making sure that the discussion stays on track. If the moderator isn't constantly keeping participants on the subject that is in front of them the group is more likely to drift off when they pursue the route of one of the most bizarre ideas.

Read Chapter 3 for guidelines for what to do in order to facilitate the discussion and other brainstorming strategies.

Start your Idea Evaluation Process if Appropriate

The process of evaluating the ideas that were generated could be completed at the conclusion of the brainstorming or following the end of the session. Plan out a strategy for evaluating the ideas prior to beginning with the session of brainstorming. If the plan calls for the evaluation to start with all the participants make sure you have a sufficient amount of time. Look up after Your Brainstorming Session for more information on the best way to go about the process of evaluating.

End your Session Well and follow-up with Participants

Certain people are quick on their feet and can come up with a variety of ideas during the brainstorming session. Some people process information more slowly and introspectively. They might require one or two days to process all the information that was thrown at them. Make sure you let everyone know that they are able to come up with new ideas once the brainstorming session is over. Make a time when the ideas will no longer be beneficial.

Thanks to the participants and inform them what they can expect from the next session. Check out the After Your Brainstorming Session for more details about what happens after your brainstorming session is over.

When your brainstorming session has concluded, you must provide your participants with feedback according to what you had told them what to anticipate.

Helping to Make Your Brainstorming Sessions More Fun and productive

A good brainstorming session is usually more productive than an ineffective one. There shouldn't be any pressure on the group members to come up with a particular number of ideas or fulfill some specific goal other than create thoughts. Pressure can hinder creativity for the majority of people. While you plan an idea-making session think about how you can make it more enjoyable. Here are some suggestions:

* Sounds, sights color, smells and colors are able to trigger different areas of the brain as well as thought processes. Utilize these stimuli to stimulate the creative process.

If you're mulling about the idea or product you have in mind having a tangible representation of the idea or product can help keep the focus of your brainstormers.

* If you're thinking about a concept you can surround your staff with colors and shapes.

* If you're mulling about the process and you are using background music to reflect the nature of the process could be suitable - for instance high-tempo music for an accelerated process, or even music that is calm for a process (such as more efficient customer service at an office for doctors).

Thinking about the marketing strategy for an item targeted at males? What about including the smell of a campfire in your plan?

You should hold your brainstorming session in a different location than the normal setting. It's surprising how much this affects the process of thinking. If the meeting is held in the same room where regularly scheduled staff meeting are being held in, the attendees will be in the "staff meeting" mentality. If, on the other hand, you're able to have the meeting in the morning in a nearby cafe and people arrive ready to relax and not to get tense. (I do not mean to suggest that your meetings for staff cause tension, but they are the best way to inquire about how things are going and giving off assignments.)

Meetings off-site for brainstorming can provide an additional benefit of eliminating distractions from your boss or colleagues with one "quick inquiry" that they want you to answer. These quick questions can derail the energy of the brainstorming session.

Make use of props to in the process of brainstorming. If you're thinking of some topical idea include the theme in the discussion by providing food, drinks, an surroundings, attire or posters, prizes etc.

For instance, if you're thinking about ways you can improve your customer experience, take pictures of your customers . Then, discuss with the group what their requirements and concerns are. Also, be cautious not to go overboard with the topic or it could distract from the brainstorming exercise.

* Offer a small amount of drinks and food - it makes the meeting more enjoyable. Make sure you don't overdo it or the food or drink could distract you from the brainstorming process.

* Have a few really innovative ideas to share with the group to start the discussion or when the ideas aren't in coming.

Give a prize to the idea that appears at first as the best innovative idea. (Remember that we're not evaluating the concepts at this point and, in the end, the idea that is creative may not be utilized. It's a way to reward creative thinking.) You could offer a variety prizes throughout the time someone has an excellent or absurd suggestion. Simply say "Give the woman a muffin to say Sara it was an awesome thought!" Don't turn the meeting into a circus, but do have fun.

Be aware that you need to keep your group focused So, only make use of sound, sights props, unconventional locations to assist your group to come up with more ideas. Do not make use of them just to make a point of it. The ability to think creatively in this area is good However, restraint is an excellent thing.

Chapter 3: Controlling Creativity Let The Fun Begin!

Brainstorming Made Easy

What is the best way to make brainstorming perform? Brainstorming is among the easiest tasks to organize and manage. Although there are many sophisticated methods of brainstorming, I've observed that simpler strategies let people concentrate on the topic for brainstorming rather than the rules or the process that the session is conducted. In the next section, I will describe the basics of brainstorming. There are additional strategies in the next chapter.

The Standard Process Standard Process

After your moderator is done his job and you've got your group and you're all set to start thinking about ideas.

The procedure is explained below. Appendix 1 contains the Brainstorming Process at-a-glance checklist. Make use of this checklist as a guide during your brainstorming session. Additionally, you can alter the procedure below by adding some of the brainstorming methods that are discussed in the next chapter.

The brainstorming topic should be presented before the entire group. (See the Preparing for Brainstorming Session for information about how to prepare your talk and the best way to deliver the topic in front of the class.)

• Inform the group on what the session is going to be executed, that is, employing the methodology that is described within this section. Appendix 1 includes Brainstorming Guidelines. You can copy these guidelines and distribute them to participants.

Instruct participants to voice their opinions on any and every idea.

• Make sure participants are aware that there is no way to tell if there is a good (or incorrect) concept to consider when brainstorming.

• Encourage participants to share ideas that aren't fully thought out. Many times, half-thoughts are fully formed once the whole group listens to the seed for an idea.

The person recording must add each idea to the list. Sometimes, using different shapes or colors can inspire more imagination. Always have a variety of colored markers available for this use.

Make sure you have ample wall space to write down your ideas.

* Don't allow criticism of your ideas. If someone says "but this would ..." be something similar to "let's take it off for now and we'll look at the best way to implement them in the future." That is a fundamental principle of brainstorming in the way it was initially invented.

Recent research has demonstrated that allowing an exchange of ideas or debate will produce more innovative ideas. If the moderator feels there's merit in taking on the argument, he/she may suggest something like "that's true but let's just jump off the idea by coming up with a different idea that addresses the issue (or which addresses the issue)." Make sure to be cautious not to get lost in a long-winded discussion of one idea until you've come up with the many original ideas you'd like to hear from the group.

If you are allowing evaluation or discussions of thoughts, make certain that the discussion isn't too negative because it will hinder the flow of ideas throughout the remainder of the meeting.

Do not permit discussion of ideas in any way, unless it is necessary to comprehend it. As mentioned above it is possible to allow additional discussion, but you should limit it to what you intend to use when brainstorming.

* Encourage people to come up with ideas, however tiny or out of the ordinary they may seem.

* Inspire the participants to not be stifled by the current process or conventional

wisdom on the subject, practicality, budgets, or their boss's preferred method of dealing with the issue.

Give yourself time to think and pondering, but keep the discussion moving swiftly. In the beginning, responses may appear a bit slow. The group must relax over a an hour or so and thoughts flow more easily.

* Once you've reached the point at which your the ideas are slowing down it is time to break the ice by beginning your discussion by asking questions that you created specifically for this reason. These questions can encourage participants to consider the subject from a different viewpoint or look at an element of the subject. Make sure not to push your brainstorming topics out of the box.

Set a flexible limit. In general, 30 to 60 minutes is an appropriate guidelines. If you're adding an evaluation time after the brainstorming process, you could prolong the duration to 70 or 80 minutes. Remember that brainstorming can be a difficult work. You shouldn't schedule or keep the session too long.

In general, you should you should end your brainstorming session after you've reached the time limit or exhausted your thoughts either way, depending on what is first. If you've exceeded your time limit , but thoughts are flowing freely Consider extending the time, but be aware that most people exhaust themselves quickly after 45 minutes of active brainstorming.

If it's appropriate, you can spend an additional 10 to 20 minutes preparing your ideas. It is sometimes better to do this by the entire group but sometimes it is done by a smaller group or just one individual. The process of organizing your ideas is covered in Chapter 4.

Make sure to conclude the brainstorming session by telling your group how the ideas they generated will be assessed and the next communication they can be expecting about the outcomes from the session of brainstorming.

Strategies for Brainstorming - beyond the basics

The basic method of brainstorming as described above can be very effective, if you regularly hold brainstorming sessions, you'll need to include an element of diversity. Alternate methods can aid in generating more ideas when brainstorming various subjects or in certain types of groups.

Alphabet Soup Style Brainstorming

I prefer this method to help me with my therapy than as method of brainstorming anytime I need to focus my attention on the events within me (like the uncomfortable health test). It can also be used for brainstorming.

Start by making sheet for your recorder that contain each one of the letters in the alphabet. It is the aim of participants in brainstorming to come up with an idea that begins with every letters of the alphabet. Don't put stress on the participants. Utilize some of the more complicated words (Q or X, perhaps) to make it more fun for the lesson, not to put pressure on them.

It is possible to approach this technique in various ways:

1.) Participants should make suggestions as they would in traditional brainstorming, while the recorder writes down the ideas in each letter in the alphabet.

2.) Invite participants to give ideas in alphabetical order. is, solicit suggestions for the letter A then B then B, etc. until you've reached Z.

3.) Begin by working your way around the participants' circle, and ask them to come up with ideas in each of the letters.

4.) Instead of working through the group, once everyone has offered their idea they may compete with anyone else within the group to give some ideas on the letters of the alphabet that they would like to see.

Keep the environment relaxed and free of pressure.

Card Shuffle Brainstorming

This technique is distinct in the sense that participants will experience quieter than typical brainstorming. Once the moderator is introduced the subject, distribute three" 5" cards to everyone. Each person should write down three or two ideas on various cards. The process should only take two minutes. After that, everyone should pass their cards to the correct.

Everyone then picks up the cards they have received pick one, then go over the idea, and finally note any ideas that they have in response to the idea that they read on their card. If they've finished with their thoughts using the card, they may move on onto the following card and repeat the same procedure. The process should take between about three or more minutes. The moderator will decide when it is appropriate to go between rounds.

Repeat the process , passing the cards they're currently holding to the left. Every person now holds cards that were written on by two or three persons. The same procedure will be followed like they did during the previous round.

Repeat the process for no more than five times but stop earlier if it appears that participants are working hard to come up with concepts.

Once the shuffling of cards has stopped and the moderator has a chance to move into a normal meeting of brainstorming, with participants sharing ideas based on the cards they're currently playing.

Circles - We Got Circles

This technique is great to brainstorm with a group and can be employed in group brainstorming. After presenting the idea to be discussed and the recorder draws circles of different sizes at various places in the idea area. Do not make the circles identical in size, and don't draw them in straight lines. The circles must be random. It is beneficial to use multiple colors. You can then ask for suggestions from people to fill in the circles. Record big ideas in big circles. If ideas aren't fully developed, the recorder may make an addition to the idea, rather than drawing the idea as a cloud.

Be sure not to judge the ideas you come up with. A thought in a huge circle isn't any better than one in a smaller circle. It's merely a method of getting ideas flowing.

From Here to From Here to Brainstorming

This technique is useful for solving problems that it is possible to identify your current location and where you'd like to be. In the presentation of the moderator, they will define the starting point (here in this instance - i.e. the place you are currently) and a final destination (there which is where you want to end up). The aim of the group is to come up with solutions that can take you from here to where you want to be.

Start by defining the location you're on a piece of paper or a sticky note. Put it at the start or on the left side of the area you want to work on. The solution should be written on a different sheet of paper or on a sticky note. Put it on the left or on the right side of your idea space. Then, you can ask the group members to complete the blank.

When ideas are created when they are generated, they must be added to the space. Some ideas could be comprehensive or global which means they travel between here and there their own. Other ideas are steps on the way between here and there. Put these ideas close the "here" and "there," depending where the idea would be placed within the process. For instance when it's an initial step, put the idea close to "here;" if it is one of the last steps, put it close to "there."

Be aware that you aren't committed to any of the ideas you put onto the Here to There board. You're brainstorming ideas like regular brainstorming. The evaluation process will be completed following the brainstorming process has been completed.

"If I were King" Brainstorming

This approach to brainstorming is in the context of the participants being able to imagine that they were the sole authority to resolve the issue that is being discussed. After the topic is presented and the moderator then asks questions such as "If you were kingof the world, what would you do to solve this problem?" It is possible to generate more ideas or look at the issue in a different way through similar inquiries. After you have received a variety of answers on the topic, you are able to encourage brainstorming based on any or all of the responses.

Here are some examples of questions:

* "If you were the king, what portion of the current system would you want to keep?"

* "If you were the king What element of the current procedure would you most definitely delete or remove?"

* "If you were King What part of the issue would you begin with?"

* "If you were the king How would you change the way you phrase the issue or topic?"

Differential Brainstorming Attracts Opposites

This approach is effective when it is incorporated into a regular brainstorming session, especially when the new ideas are fading away. The idea is to look at the issue, topic or issue from a different direction or on the other side. For instance, if the issue was to increase the amount of traffic on a website You could say "Imagine that we were getting too lots of website traffic. What was we doing to gain it?"

Simply Say It! Brainstorming

In this manner it is the role of moderator to (or the other members) invite participants to "Just Say that!" After presenting the idea to be brainstormed and beginning a typical meeting for brainstorming, the moderator notices that some of the participants hesitate because of anxiety, fear of not being right or perhaps not having a fully thought-out idea in their heads. The moderator turns to the participant and then says "Just be yourself!" encouraging the participant to speak whatever comes into their head. Once the group has gotten the message and they see the expression at the other participants when they're on the edge of an idea, but are hesitant to share it and challenge each other to "Just Say it!"

Mind Mapping

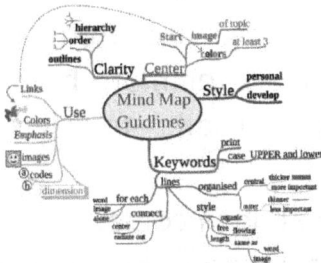

A Mind Map for the Mind Guidelines
(c) User: Nicoguaro (c) User: Nicoguaro Wikimedia Commons (c) User: Nicoguaro / Wikimedia Commons CC-BY-SA-3.0

Mind mapping refers to the act of drawing a sequence of thoughts that are related as illustrated by the above mind map. (Note that the mind map above is quite organized. Mind maps created by freehand are typically not so "pretty.") Mind maps can be used to facilitate brainstorming since it visually depicts the random process and the result of brainstorming. It's a mix of the scientific and the imaginative and is perfect for brainstorming , and particularly useful in brainstorming by yourself. A mind map typically includes a central idea that every other idea branches. Other thoughts and ideas can originate from the primary thought or one or more branches. Colors are often used to link concepts thematically.

Each time an idea comes up then add it to your mental map using a pencil to draw a line around the idea that served as the basis for the original idea. Your mind map could appear like this.

Although he didn't invent the concept of "mind mapping,"" British psychologist and author Tony Buzan is credited with popularizing the concept in the 1970s early. When I first heard of minds maps my initial reaction was to think that these were merely lines that were radiated from the central point instead of radiating from top to bottom. This is the basic idea however Buzan will argue that an outline requires users to absorb the content by reading starting from the left and from top to the bottom. Buzan along with other brain scientists have discovered that we browse through entire pages in a non-linear manner.

Personally I'm the linear top to bottom, left-to-right and top to bottom type of reader. However, I've found mind mapping to be useful for organizing subjects that had me tearing my outline. In the same way, they can be useful for brainstorming.

There are many software programs that aid in mind mapping. Below are two easy and cheap (or free) software programs to help you mind map:

http://www.mindapp.com/ - This is the software I use. It's affordable and easy to use.

http://www.mindmeister.com/ - A free software that is simple and highly rated.

There are other options available. Google "mind mapping application" and "mind mapping software review" to find out more.

Speed Round Brainstorming

This technique could be intimidating for some participants. It's best for those who have highly energetic, quick-thinkers and not easily scared.

The purpose of speed round brainstorming is to discover the best ideas within a specific amount of time.

The moderator will announce during the presentation the amount of ideas or time to be used for speed round sessions. Once the moderator is finished with their presentation, the clock begins and participants can shout their ideas as fast as they can.

A second recorder can help rapid brainstorming sessions to ensure you have recorded every idea coming up

An alternative to this method is to provide participants with the opportunity for a brief period to brainstorm speedily independently, and write down their own thoughts, and then start the standard brainstorming. Participants are able to share their thoughts they came up with during their own speed-round brainstorming during the regular brainstorming session.

Similar to this, you can break the entire group down into three or two smaller groups, and conduct the brainstorming session in a sprint and then bring the entire group together for a regular brainstorming session.

Brainstorming for Split Personality

This technique challenges participants to look at the subject from different angles. In the initial phase of preparation the moderator will define the various roles that people play in the discussion. For instance, let's imagine you're brainstorming ways to improve your product, for instance. People involved include bosses, customers, factory workers, suppliers marketing personnel, salesmen, etc. The identification of these roles is a initial step in the brainstorming process with your team.

Then, you can continue thinking in a more normal manner, while ensuring that everyone thinks about the issue in the context of their own viewpoint. If you decide to do this it is possible to assign a section of the idea board for each position instead of listing every idea in one list.

Another option is to ask your brainstormers to group up according to their roles over a period of time. Each group should have an organizer to record their thoughts. Then , bring the group together, and write down your ideas. Then, hold a brainstorming session where participants are free to step out of their roles and offer suggestions from any angle.

"What If" Brainstorming

This technique alters the actuality of the issue by asking "What do you think if? ..." You can answer this question by eliminating one of the elements of the issue or some of the ideas that you brainstormed. For example, if you are designing the packaging for the launch of a new product, we might consider asking "What is the best option if cardboard wasn't an alternative?" or "What if the product needed to be handled with care?" If one of the most popular suggestions was to pack the product using molded rubber, you could ask "What If that were too expensive ? What alternatives can you think of?" Or conversely "What do we do if we want to take up the ante and enhance

the look of it and more appealing? What
ideas like that do exist?"

Chapter 4: Keeping The Fruit Of Your Imagination

Following Your Brainstorming Sessio

After you've completed the brainstorming session and brainstorming, it's time to analyze the ideas in a more objective manner. Naturally, there was an intention to identify the most fresh and innovative ideas as is possible. The next step is to analyze the ideas and determine what ideas to examine further. The review process involves the process of categorizing, mixing, condensing or expanding and refining ideas. The process will result in an assessment of which ideas to further analyze and/or apply.

Before beginning with your session of brainstorming, determine whether you'd like the entire group to assist in this exercise, a smaller portion of the brainstorming team or one specific member of your team (often as moderator). If the entire group is going to participate, make sure to keep the meeting shorter or schedule an extra meeting to facilitate this.

Make sure to share the results of your brainstorming session as well as the evaluation and subsequent implementation of the ideas to the people who took part in the brainstorming session.

Use these guidelines to assess the ideas that were generated during brainstorming sessions:

Pre-Evaluation

Following you have had your session of brainstorming, look over your notes to make sure they are clear and comprehensive enough to allow you to recall the concepts you had when you return to them after having them set aside for a few hours or longer. Take about 30 minutes making notes that are more complete as you need to.

Notes should be set aside for at least a night. Based on your personal style the process of brainstorming can be exhausting or energizing. It is not advisable to begin the process of evaluation with either of these conditions.

If you're already exhausted out of your energy reserves, you're likely to pick options that require minimum effort, not the most efficient suggestions.

If you're feeling upbeat You may choose ideas that are too broad or that resonate with you emotionally, but aren't practical.

Organize Your List

When you have set those notes to one side for an hour or so, look over the list briefly and combine items which are just different ways to say the same thing, or ideas that are so similar that you couldn't possibly do each without. If the list you created from the brainstorming session isn't overly messy and "ugly" you might be able complete this goal by circling similar items and drawing arrows. You're likely to find yourself revising (or typing) the list in the process. (There's no problem with messy lists, they're usually the result of a effective brainstorming session.)

The next step is to arrange your list of ideas in a manner that fits the project. This requires a small amount of assessment, but not a complete analysis of the concepts.

For instance the time we release books for our clients We organize a marketing brainstorming meeting together with clients. The goal for the session to brainstorm is create concepts from which we create a the most unique marketing plan. After a brainstorming session we create a long list of concepts as follows:

general ideas - concepts that can be used with any other avenues for marketing

Tier 1 Ideas ideas that are the most appealing to the writer

Ideas from Tier 2. that have high potential, however, the writer doesn't have as much enthusiasm to pursue.

Tier 3 Concepts - ideas which required the most time cost, the most expensive, or in which the writer is least inclined to put into practice

There's nothing special about this arrangement, except that it was suitable to the product and customer. The concept could just be put in this order:

Ideas for Pre-Release

Ideas to implement in the very first thirty days

Ideas for implementing days 31 - 60

etc.

If the brainstorming session you had was about something that you work on it is possible to use a Tier 1 Tier 2, Tier 3 method but alter the descriptions so that they relate to the cost and ease of implementation, and how quickly it would bring in revenue or improve customer satisfaction or what levels of approvals could be required for implementing them.

Another method of organizing the outcomes of a corporate brainstorming session is to organize the ideas in the departments that will implement the concept.

The way you organize your list will have all to do with the way in which implementation will be carried out and who will do it. The aim of this process is to go through your lengthy collection of thoughts and arrange them in a way that you are able to begin to analyze the ideas.

In our scenario we were creating the marketing plan to be executed by the writer The best way to approach it was to conclude the brainstorming session by conducting an informal review of the concepts with the client and ask her to evaluate the ideas on a scale from between one and four. This helped us create an effective marketing strategy that was the most suitable for her , based on the ideas that came up in the brainstorming session.

Assess and implement

After putting together the list of ideas it's now time to narrow this down to manageable list that only includes ideas that merit further scrutiny. This could be done by one person (often acting as moderator) working by themselves or in the help of a small group (some of whom might have been part of this brainstorming exercise). The final result of this process will be an outline of ideas you can use your time effort to critically examine.

Don't discard your original list You never know when you'll decide to implement certain ideas that you originally thought were not worth exploring.

Pick five ideas that interest you most. You can then flesh out those five ideas by researching how they can have to be executed, the potential benefits would be, and what the price would be, etc. The information you gather will allow you to make a final decision regarding which ideas you want to implement. When you come to a blocked street, you can either stop the idea and pick a new one or plan a more focused brainstorming session that focuses on clearing the avenue.

Based on the reason for your brainstorming, you can go back to the ideas and go through them individually to choose the best or collaborate together to select the most effective ideas.

It could be helpful to form an ensemble of people who have an experience or personality that is similar that of the individual who came up with the idea that was the most successful in the initial brainstorming session. This new group of people who have similar, not different backgrounds, could assist in helping "drill down" into some really imaginative and innovative ideas within the same thought process.

Use the best ideas or concepts. Your brainstorming session has achieved its purpose by providing fresh and new ideas that led to improvements in a particular area of your life or your job!

Engage With Your Brainstorming Team

* If your group is not involved in the process of evaluation, give feedback to them as necessary. This will be a way to reward them for the time they have spent in support of the event and will encourage them to take part during future sessions of brainstorming.

Chapter 5: Brainstorming, Party Of One

When You Do Not Have a Group

If you are unable to find someone to brainstorm with There are a variety of techniques that can help you start brainstorming while working on your own. The principle is similar - your aim is to brainstorm as many ideas as you can. There is no evaluation of your concepts you brainstorm. Make it a point to come up with at minimum five completely outrageous ideas that will allow you to step outside of your box. (Remember that there is not to put yourself under pressure. The purpose of the goal is to free yourself from keeping within the boundaries of practicality. If the goal is a source of pressure on your own brainstorming, do not go there!)

As the process of coming up with new ideas is a method of leading us to new places when we don't have anything to re-inspire us Start by writing down the topic you're planning to think. This will allow you to come back when you've wandered away from the goal. Be aware that you'll play the roles of moderator as well as the recorder and brainstormer when working on your own. This is more than enough costumes for a single afternoon!

To help you see the subject in a different way to help you see the topic from a different angle, grab 4 sheets of white paper (or make use of four areas on whiteboards as well as four windows on your monitor or monitor, etc.). On on the uppermost part of the sheet or space write a few sentences to identify the viewpoint that you'll take a look at the topic.

If, for instance, you're brainstorming ideas to write a book You could choose four options on the list below:

Things you are aware of quite a bit about

Things that you are interested in

* Things you aren't sure anything about, but would like to learn more about or find out more about

* The most frequently asked questions your coworkers, customers, or managers might ask.

There are topics which everyone is writing about today

Topics that no one appears to write about at the moment

The following topics could be relevant to your work-related life

Possible topics related to your family life

Experiences from the past that may be the basis for a novel

Choose one of the four options from the list above , and begin writing or typing your list, without regard to how great the ideas are. Within a half hour you should be in a position to think of 40 or 50 ideas!

Make sure you write down any thoughts that aren't complete thoughts. For instance, I tried individual brainstorming using the same method to brainstorm ideas for an article. I chose the three initial perspectives from the list, and the final option. Then I began to come to ideas. One of the thoughts I wrote down under "things I don't know much regarding" was "some technological area?" No specific area of technology came to my mind however I could tell that there were areas that I would consider writing about. That's why I recorded it. I will revisit it to revisit the subject and then do the same level of brainstorming ideas on different aspects of technology that I can write about.

Check out the strategies in Chapter 3 to get additional ideas that could add some creativity to your brainstorming efforts.

After about 30 minutes Take some time out, grab the perfect cup of Starbucks mix, then then check your email. You can then go back at your to-do list, and get started on choosing those five options that interest you most.

The process of brainstorming involves Thinking Outside the Box to create a different outcome

It can take some time to brainstorm ideas however the rewards are huge. People who think creatively are able to create ideas to solve problems, generate new ideas, and spark new enthusiasm.

When you brainstorm with a group or on your own or whatever method you employ, have fun with the process! Brainstorming can be more enjoyable than working!

Appendices Index

Identifying your Participants and Moderators

Moderator Requirements Checklist

Checklist for Presentation

Brainstorming Process at-a-Glance (Moderator's Checklist)

Appendix 2 Appendix 2 Brainstorming Guidelines

Identifying your Participants and Moderators

3 - 6 people

Varying backgrounds

"[] Many experiences

Varieties of personalities or personality types

2 to 4 people who are at ease with each other

1 2 people who don't have any acquaintances with each other.

Then...

Select a Moderator

~~~~~~~~~~~~~~~~

Potential Participants

1.

2.

3.

4.

5.

6.

Alt 1.

Alt 2.

Alt 3.

Potential Moderators

1.

2.

Things to Consider when Choosing the Moderator

The Moderator is accountable of the following things:

* Choosing the best approach or method

The presentation should be prepared.

* Preparing questions to stimulate imagination

* Creating creative ideas to present during the discussion

* Preparing the location

* Inviting group members

* Gathering materials

* Selecting an audio recorder

Prepared for Post-Brainstorming exercises

* Presenting the subject to the group

The flow and flow can be altered in the brainstorming

* Closing the session with a good note
* Follow-up with participants
* The process of evaluating ideas

Moderator Responsibilities Checklist

Get ready for the session

Choose the best method or approach

Create the presentation

Answer questions that inspire imagination

[ ] Come up with some creative concepts regarding the subject

Preparing the venue

Explore ways to make your session more enjoyable and productive

Invite group members

Gather the necessary items

Select an audio recorder

Get ready for post-brainstorming exercises

Choose the recorder

The tasks are unique in your Brainstorming Session

The Brainstorming Session

( ) Present the topic to the group

[Moderate the flow

Inspire creativity by asking questions or sharing your thoughts

Start evaluating ideas if needed at this point.

[ ] Finish the session properly

Unique tasks in your Brainstorming Session

Following the Brainstorming Session

( ) Follow-up with participants

Begin the process of evaluating ideas

The tasks are unique in your Brainstorming Session

Checklist for Presentation

Be concise up to 3 sentences.

(a) Define the problem the issue, topic or issue - what's the goal in the discussion?

Restate the issue using a somewhat different manner.

Give the time to answer questions during your presentation of the subject.

Create one or two questions to start the discussion.

Create a variety of questions that will encourage creativity during the meeting.

[ ] Create several ideas that are off the wall to stimulate the imagination.

Brainstorming Process In-A-Glance (Moderator's Checklist)

The discussion topic in front of the entire members of the group (use to use the Presentation Checklist).

(Explain the guidelines for brainstorming sessions (use Brainstorming Guidelines).

Choose the recorder option if you have not previously done this.

The person recording should include every suggestion to the list.

[Encourage participants to make a noise with any and every idea.

Remind participants that there's no any such thing as a bad (or incorrect) concept in brainstorming.

Instruct participants to share ideas that aren't fully realized.

Do not allow any criticism to the concepts. If you allow critique, make sure that the tone of the meeting is positive.

In general, do not allow discussions of ideas except for what is necessary to know about it.

Inspire participants to not to be shackled by current procedures and conventional wisdom budgets, or the way their boss prefers to approach.

Give yourself time for thought and pondering, but keep the discussion moving quickly.

Use your planned questions or suggestions to keep the flow of ideas in motion.

Be aware of your time limit. Typically 30 to 60 minutes.

Generally, you should end your brainstorming session once you've exceeded your time limit or have exhausted all your ideas depending on what comes first.

If it's suitable, you can spend another 10 to 20 minutes organising your ideas.

Then, end the session of brainstorming by explaining to your group how your ideas will be evaluated, and the future communications participants should anticipate.

Brainstorming Ideas for Guidelines

The purpose for brainstorming is create as many fresh, new and innovative ideas on the subject as is possible. Following the moderator's presentation, the participant has discussed the issue, the issue or subject...

It will then add each suggestion to the list.

* Tweet out any and all thoughts.

* There isn't a anything as a bad thought in brainstorming.

* Don't be timid! Keep in mind that there isn't way to tell if you've got a good or good idea to brainstorm.

Don't be influenced by the current process traditional wisdom, common sense practicality, budgets, or the way your boss prefers to do things.

* Make suggestions that aren't practical.

* Make suggestions that are impossible to put into practice.

* Communicate ideas that are culturally unorthodox or are counter-intuitive.

* Express ideas that aren't fully developed. Others can fill the gap.

In general, don't be critical of ideas when they are proposed.

* If you're attracted to criticize the idea, look for alternatives to the concept.

In general, don't discuss concepts when they are proposed or questioned, unless you are required to comprehend the concept.

Are you feeling overwhelmed? Put your head down and block out all the other thoughts for a few minutes. You can think about the topic. After that, you can join the group and share your thoughts.

* If you've got an idea that you want to share after the session has ended you can communicate this idea with the moderator.

Chapter 6: The Brainstorming Process Tools And Techniques

Since its inception during the 1940s' early years the practice of brainstorming has been a crucial method for generating ideas. In the course of time, new variations of the traditional brainstorming process are created in order to eliminate the negatives of brainstorming in groups. Today, there are numerous methods and tools to help facilitate and manage brainstorming sessions. No matter if you're planning to discuss ideas face-to-face or via the internet, tools for brainstorming can help you generate more ideas, as well as gather and organize them effectively.

What are brainstorming tools and methods? We're not talking about basics like pen and whiteboard, or even a piece of paper. In this chapter, we'll explore ways to approach the issue from various perspectives, frame the appropriate questions, improve collaboration between participants, increase engagement, and come up with the most innovative ideas feasible. One of the major topics that we will cover in the chapter are virtual or online brainstorming tools. They are extremely valuable in the current movement towards remote work. They enable digitization of the entire idea-generation process and also working together without sacrificing your individuality.

Chapter 2 described the traditional method of brainstorming and its roots as well as the principles and rules in depth. This chapter will examine the main flaws in traditional brainstorming, and provide ten main variations of traditional brainstorming, and present X other methods for generating ideas that are based on the traditional brainstorming methods. The subsequent chapters will employ these tools to explain how to set the right group or personal brainstorming sessions.

The drawbacks of traditional Brainstorming

Do these scenarios look familiar? Your team leader or manager is asking you to participate in a tense exercise that is called a brainstorming session. They invite participants to "think outside the box" and then wait for you along with the other members of the team to experience a eureka moment and create brilliant ideas that previously had no one thought of! Unfortunately, many traditional brainstorming sessions suffer from an absence of organization and planning and goals that are unclear, divergent thinking, and only some dominant speakers, with others sitting silently through the majority or all of the session. In many businesses, brainstorming sessions are more of "a tick-box" event with no concrete results. The most common issues that arise during brainstorming are behavior and group interaction and are more prevalent in business teams in start-ups and corporations. Corporate politics can also be obstacles to the free flow of creation of ideas. Also, certain people might concentrate on what the boss would like to hear.

As we mentioned in Chapter 2 Brainstorming sessions need the right planning and facilitation. In the absence of this, they could yield only a few or even no outcomes. Let's look at some of the most frequent problems with traditional brainstorming. We'll then discuss ways to avoid them and what innovative methods are available to avoid these traps.

1. Production Blocking

Production blocking occurs when an person blocks or hinders other participants in an informal discussion. In the example above in a brainstorming session, if the group is comprised of six participants and one person presents their idea and the remaining five have been "blocked" and are unable to offer their own input. This means that they are likely to not have enough time to brainstorm fresh ideas or be distracted and forget their thoughts before they get the chance to present the ideas with others. The majority of people are unable to come up with new ideas when they are listening to another sharing their idea. Production blockage becomes more difficult when the size of the group brainstorming expands. We can overcome this issue by allowing people to draft their ideas prior to taking part in the discussion which will prevent the possibility of "blocking" in the brainstorming session.

2. Evaluation Apprehension

This is the normal anxiety that comes from speaking up about the wild or crazy ideas. Before people even start to speak they wonder that what would others consider? This can stop people from taking off on tangents and reduces the number of ideas can be evaluated by the group after your brainstorm session. So, even with guidelines for brainstorming fears of getting judged could be a significant barrier to solving creative problems. The fear of self-censorship can lead to self-censorship and a decrease in the effectiveness of brainstorming. The problem, however, is usually solved with innovative techniques like Brainwriting.

3. Topic Fixation

Someone has come with an amazing idea, and then everyone is convinced that there is no alternative idea that could be more superior. Therefore, even during the meeting, everyone's brain remains focused on the subject, which in turn narrows the possibilities of other ideas. It's like the participants are thinking, "We've already come to an agreement therefore why should we pitch a new concept?" This problem has been identified and resolved using different methods of brainstorming, such as Brainwriting, the Step Ladder or Brainwriting.

4. Dominant Personalities

Have you met anyone who has such a strong personality? They are able to be in a room and everything they say appears to be solid. When they leave it's hard to believe that the concept is unusual, but you find yourself agreeing with the idea because the person who thought up the idea is persuasive. People with strong personalities control the room in the beginning of the session , and they keep their dominance throughout the session.

Unfortunately, brainstorming sessions that are traditional frequently fall victim to this trap. Certain participants are enough convincing to easily influence the group's opinions and block any avenues for creativity. Effective facilitation techniques and facilitation methods like brainwriting or mind mapping can help to overcome this problem.

5. Anonymity: The Lack of Anonymity

A common fear among participants of brainstorming groups is the face-to face format of the meeting. It's not just about fearing that people will mock your idea. It's also a concern that they'll accuse you of creating it at all. Despite the group method of thinking about ideas, there's occasions where ideas, whether bad or otherwise could be located to one individual. This is why it's normal for people to stifle their unconventional ideas since they are easily assigned to them. This issue can be resolved with anonymous brainstorming techniques like brain-netting.

6. Too Many Cooks

Are you aware of the rumors about the over-cooking of cooks? The traditional method of brainstorming could also be affected by this issue. An unbalanced group of participants can cause chaos, which creates a challenge to organize ideas. Everybody can be speaking simultaneously or even not, it could take a lot of time for everyone to contribute. Limiting the number of participants taking part or deciding the people who will participate based on their skills could help to solve this issue.

In the last few years, numerous people and companies have tried to fix the problems that were mentioned earlier. The result is a broad variety of brainstorming techniques that employ various approaches and thematic areas of focus. The remainder in this section will explore twelve innovative brainstorming methods. These methods are based on the fundamental concepts of group synergy as well as divergent-convergent thinking, but each with its own unique twist.

Questions to be posed

Created by Hal Gregersen of the MIT Sloan School of Management Questionstorming is a method of thinking about questions. The principle behind the concept is that an open, fresh and honest inquiry can lead to fresh insights, and allows you to explore unexplored territory. Questionstorming can be more efficient than traditional brainstorming since it lets people think about the issue by asking questions, rather than searching for answers. As we have discussed earlier in this chapter, evaluation anxiety is a major drawback of traditional brainstorming. People are under pressure when trying to discover the "right" solution. If they're worried about finding that perfect "right" solution they are more likely to keep back to avoid looking dumb.

Questionstorming has many benefits when compared to traditional brainstorming. The primary benefit is that, since you may not have the correct answer, you'll not feel obligated to just make suggestions that appear to be the right ones. This feeling of freedom leads to an environment that is more enjoyable and offers greater opportunities to come up with innovative concepts. Another benefit of question-forming is that it allows you to redefine the original question. Do you recall the examples from Chapter 2? You can see the way it can have a major impact when the question is "How can we create bridges on the water?" or "How can we traverse this water?" If the brainstorming session begins with the construction of bridges without asking about the specific issue in hand (i.e. cross the river) it's possible that the result will not be the best. A focus solely on asking questions prevents participants from jumping to the answer or focusing on the possibility of a solution. This can eventually broaden the possibilities of ideas and finally asking questions can be enjoyable and anyone is able to do it.

Gregersen developed his question-smattering method by relying on two key rules:

1. The only questions allowed are The facilitator should direct anyone who attempts to offer solutions or respond to other's questions.

2. Preambles or justifications are not allowed. This is in order to avoid framing questions and helping people understand the issue in a particular manner.

He also suggested certain guidelines for question-storming sessions. Here are a few examples:

* Utilize conventional methods of divergent thinking (such like making random connections) to uncover new questions.

Begin with basic questions before moving on to more sophisticated ones.

* Questions shouldn't make people feel uncomfortable and create an atmosphere of terror, or provoke.

* Multiple sessions of questionstorming are generally more efficient than a single long session.

Questionstorming should begin with a focus on the number of questions. Sorting, analysis and prioritizing are the next steps.

Over the years, Gregersen created a standard question-stacking method for groups and individual brainstorming sessions. The method has been used in hundreds of teams from various companies, such as Chanel, Danone, Disney, Fidelity, Salesforce, and many non-profit organisations and individuals. Here's how questionstorming works:

Step 1. Setting the Stage

Everything begins with a statement, as opposed to an inquiry. For instance, when using brainstorming, you begin the discussion by asking: "How can we increase our customer base?" With questionstorming, however, the statement that opens the discussion usually reads "We require more customers." Do you notice the distinction?

Step 2: List the Questions

After you've settled on the statement you want to make The following step is to begin asking questions relevant to the topic. This can be done the same manner as ideas were discussed during brainstorming. Participants are given a predetermined period of time in which they can list as many possible questions in response to the specific question. Let's take for instance, the statement was originally"we need more customers. The following questions could include:

What are some of our clients?

What's the demographic profile of our clients?

* Can we grow our customers?

We have how many clients do we currently have?

* How much more could we increase our customers?

* What is it that makes our clients like us?

* Are we able to support more customers?

The benefit of this approach is the fact that asking questions is usually simpler than finding the answers. It's not a requirement to think about it and go in to your You just need to be inquisitive. An effective method for conducting this exercise is to allow participants 10 minutes to think of the most questions they can think of. But, you could start interrupting them around 8 minutes and asking participants to think of 10 more questions. This method will help ensure that they've covered all the possible possibilities instead of doing nothing during the last couple of minutes or just letting it go.

Step 3: Modifying the questions

If you are tweaking the question, you should make it a closed question to one that is closed, and the reverse. Closed questions are one that can be answered with either a yes or no. Open questions require an explanation, or explanation. For instance, in the previous example the closed question is How can we help more customers? If we could open that question, the answer would be: How do help us support more customers? Switching the question from open to closed version also helps to set the stage for future subsequent questions. Let's revisit the previous example. Do we have the capacity to serve more customers? If yes then "How can we assist additional customer?" is the logical next question. But what happens if you don't know the answer? In the event that your answer turns out to be no it is then going on to the open question isn't required. A new open-ended question might be asked, for instance: "How can we improve our capability to provide better support to the needs of more clients?"

If you change the words and you will get a completely different perspective on the subject. This helps you get more questions, and consequently, expands the range of the concept.

Step 4 Step 4: Sorting and Prioritizing the Questions

Making the decision to ask questions could be considered the phase of divergent thinking in the process. This is the time to connect all your thoughts. After prioritizing your thoughts and putting them in your converging thinking stage. Now you'll have to identify the questions that help to reframe the issue and might provide a new path. It is recommended that you examined the chosen questions to determine what makes them relevant or crucial. Then, you must commit to following at least one additional avenue in response to your chosen questions. This is the time when you will be able to begin answering the questions.

The similarities between the technique of brainstorming of Alex Osborn and the questionstorming method by Hal Gregersen is interesting. Both approach the issue from two different perspectives however, they follow the same guidelines. The process of question-scrambling can be carried out either in a group or on its own either face to face or via online. The basic principles and stages remain the same. However, the process requires some adjustments in order to best fit the environment.

What-If-I-Should-I-Do Questions

"If you're not sure of what you'd do if you had the freedom to be as free as you like Then how do you know what you would do under a set of constraints?" That was what Professor Russel Ackoff, a professor at the Wharton School, University of Pennsylvania declared. "What-If" questions force us to think. They help us escape the current reality and lead us into a realm in which anything is possible. It's a great way to prepare our minds to think creatively or come up with ideas that we've never thought of before.

"What-If" questions give you an opportunity to enter an attitude of someone who is unhinged or unencumbered by the limitations of the box. If you're looking to stretch your "out out of your box" thinking muscles, then asking"what-if" questions are an ideal method to begin. The purpose of these questions is to make the team "ready" to think beyond the norm. These are "what is if" questions:

What If we were to have an unlimitable budget?

What happens if children take the majority of our decisions?

What do we do if we let our customers create the project?

* What if we were able to market this product in an entirely different market?

* What if we were to sell our entire range directly on the internet?

These questions can be an excellent way to start off insight that may result in creative solutions. The great thing about this method is that it lets you visualize seemingly unreal situations in order to prompt you to think about how you can tackle those scenarios. It opens up the door to the imagination. With your imagination open you may smash the box.

"What is the scenario" questions can be viewed as warm-up exercises, making them an ideal activity for a team who is novice to brainstorming. In addition, if they're having trouble finding innovative ideas using "what-if" questions can help guide the team into an even more imaginative mental state. Similar to other brainstorming methods It is recommended to devote some time to the planning at the beginning as well as the facilitation discussions or sessions.

Mind Mapping

Inventions in the 1960s by Tony Buzan in the 1960s Mind mapping is a method of creating an image representation of your thoughts. It is not about creating illustrations or caricatures of ideas. Instead, the emphasis is on identifying connections between the ideas arranged around a particular subject or question. Mind mapping is akin to it's a flowchart. However, it may not be as well organized like a traditional flowchart. Association and creativity play an important role in how concepts and ideas are linked. The mental representation of mind mapping can also incorporate diverse shapes, colors and patterns.

Mind mapping is an exercise in visuals which helps you understand the connections between various aspects of a challenge. For instance when a business is trying to cut operating expenses A mind map can assist in finding connections between the various things that consume funds. In a printing business for instance paper usage can be a significant cost-driver. What are the factors that influence the use of paper? What amount of paper is used up every day? How can you reduce the amount of paper wasted? Are there times when paper usage is higher than normal? Why? What is happening on those days? And what can you do to control the events? These are just a few of the aspects which mind maps can assist to in organising and narrowing down by establishing connections and presenting them visually.

In general, this method is best if

1. You're trying to discover connections and connections between various concepts and concepts.

2. You're trying to mix and match various concepts.

3. You should establish a systematic approach for an assignment or topic.

Here are the most common steps to map your mind:

Step 1: Selecting an appropriate Medium

Begin by figuring out the tools you'll use to map your mind. For instance, you could utilize a pen and paper as well as a whiteboard, blackboard, post-it notepads, or even a laptop or tablet using mind mapping software like Simplemind and MindNode.

Step 2: Place the Central Theme in the Central

Start by putting your main topic at the center of the page. All subsequent writing you do should have some connection to this main subject. Let's take an example: your goal is losing weight in a healthy way. Place "healthy fat loss" on the top of your page.

Step 3: Locating Subtopics

The next step is to figure out the subtopics that fall under weight loss. What are the key elements to losing weight? Of course, diet and exercises. What else is there? In addition, you need to consider the amount of rest you get and your stress levels and the way you position yourself in the menstrual cycle of women. It is also possible to include your current weight as well as your desired weight. Then, arrange the subtopics in relation to the core issue and connect them by lines. Following that, it is time adding further ideas in relation with the topics.

If you're focusing on "exercise" as an area of study, you could think of different forms of exercise to shed weight. For instance, walking ten thousand steps per day, biking between work and home or dog walking, for example. What amount of physical activity do you do now? And what can you do to increase it?

Write down any similar ideas within the topic. For instance:

* Walking ten thousand times which is equivalent to five miles a day, is an excellent starting place.

How can I count my daily steps? Set up a step count application on my phone, or opt for the fitness band.

* What exercises should I do?

* Walking, jogging, cycling, swimming, HIIT, yoga, etc.

You can then list the related concepts related to eating habits:

The ideal calorie intake daily is two thousand calories for males and one thousand five hundred calories for females.

* How do I count my calories?

* Different diet regimens like Ketogenic Diet or Intermittent Fasting.

5. Connecting and Creating Connections

It's now time to identify connections and relationships between diverse subtopics. It is important to determine the ways in which one topic is connected to the other and how you can utilize the information to reach the end target. For instance, you could connect the two things: diet and exercise. Food is about taking calories, while exercise is about burning the calories. The most important factor in losing weight is eating less calories than you burn. Therefore, why not keep track of your calories consumption to be sure you're eating less and doing adequate exercise that burns off specific amount of calories? That's the connection.

This is a basic example of using mind mapping. You can however make use of the same method to tackle more difficult issues. The benefit of Mind mapping is the fact that it's not limited to only verbal information. If it's helpful to add images with the subtopics, include some colors and experiment with the map when you are looking to keep things interesting.

Brainwriting

Brainwriting is an alternative to the traditional brainstorming method that is designed to solve many of the problems with brainstorming that were mentioned previously in the chapter. Utilizing this technique it is possible to generate many ideas while strengthening relationships between these ideas.

The brainwriting process is easy and instead of expressing your thoughts verbally, record them and then pass them on. There are several variations of brainwriting. The first step is to look at the benefits of brainstorming, and how it can enhance traditional brainstorming. After that, we'll review the most popular brainwriting strategies.

Researchers have discovered that brainwriting can help people become creative, without anxiety about performance or evaluation anxiety, personality, politics, or production blockage. Therefore, a planned and managed brainwriting session can produce innovative ideas. Let's look at how brainwriting can be useful for brainstorming ideas:

1. Because the participants don't have to be in groups, they will not suffer from anxiety about performance. Speaking in public is a challenge in many individuals, which makes people so nervous that they may repress their thoughts completely. The dynamics in the group and human emotions can create a worse anxiety. Eye-rolling, mumbled remarks, or even seeing create a toxic atmosphere during conventional brainstorming meetings. There's a lot less room for these actions when you write your ideas down since there is no chance for the group to react to any written suggestion.

2. A lot of workplaces have too much internal politics. It can manifest itself during brainstorming sessions with rivalries and alliances among the participants, which can affect the quality of the output and harming morale. Brainwriting is a way to manage such political issues because everyone creates

their own thoughts privately and in a non-public manner.

3. Brainwriting lets participants communicate their thoughts in the highest degree of privacy, as well as completely private in large groups or via online brainwriting. This allows the most shy and shy members of the group to feel comfortable and share their thoughts without anxiety of being considered a failure.

4. Production blocking is the primary flaw in traditional brainstorming. With brainwriting, participants don't need to wait around to get their turn. They can all record their thoughts at the same time. Therefore, brainwriting is particularly ideal for large groups to creating a variety of ideas more quickly. Additionally that when everyone is creating their thoughts simultaneously and everyone isn't "pre-empted" by another's similar thought. Brainwriting also allows users to discuss their ideas in a short period of time, without having to call an appointment.

This is a great option to team members working in various time zones.

5. Brainwriting is a much more flexible method than traditional brainstorming. It can be conducted in a group , or by one person, simultaneously or over time with anonymity and without anxiety of being assessed. Additionally, because the thoughts are recorded and not lost in conversations and are more organized. Furthermore, building off of the other's ideas is easier feasible since people record their comments. In the end, after several rounds, all the paths that an idea's taken becomes evident, which makes it much easier to connect ideas and create combinations.

Brainstorming comes in many variations which are all based on the exact principles, but each has their own method and appropriate for specific circumstances. As with traditional brainstorming, you should always to establish the conditions for

We will go over the four kinds of brainwriting

Basic Writing

After setting the stage and supplying participants with the necessary details about the subject the facilitator will then present the questions they would like participants to respond to and then asks them to write their thoughts in writing on smaller index cards and post-it notes. The facilitator is also expected to explain the fundamental guidelines. For example, the length of time, requirements, and limitations, like the concept is feasible to implement, without spending any more money.

Participants will be given a certain amount of time to draft their thoughts. The time available is typically restricted, for example, a couple of minutes. This prevents participants from going over all the details or giving reasons for their thoughts. After all ideas have been gathered and compiled with the help of the facilitator. After that, participants look over their ideas and pick the most effective ones.

Interactive Brainwriting

This method follows the same basic principles of the basic brainwriting. Instead of putting together all the thoughts, every participant passes their post-it notes or cards to the other team participant. Everyone makes remarks or comments on the cards prior to passing them to the next participant. The process can continue for as many rounds you'd like. Brainwriting is a method that lets participants collaborate on ideas like what occurs in traditional brainstorming. The only distinction in the process is that interaction doesn't include conversations.

Collaborative Brainwriting

Collaborative brainwriting functions the same way as regular brainwriting, but more freely and with more flexibility. It is usually a matter of having a large sheet of paper with markers as well as post-it notes placed in an open area that is open to everyone. The facilitator writes down the issue or question on the top of the page and then invites participants to record their thoughts when they are at an idea. The ideas may be original or based on others ideas. Facilitators can establish an end date to gather all notes, then sort through, review, and write them down.

6-3-5 Brainwriting

This method is most effective when larger groups are present, and can be split into six groups. The fundamental principle is that six people create three ideas each round. Each round lasts about five minutes (hence the name 6-3-5).

After the groups have been established, hand each participant an e-form that has the problem you are trying to solve at the top. There are additional boxes below the question for them to fill in the ideas. The aim is to get three ideas for each round. Therefore, the precise number of ideas boxes will depend upon the amount of rounds.

In the first round participants write down three ideas. In The second session, form is handed to the next member of the team who is able to read the initial three ideas, and then writes down a third set of ideas. They may be entirely new ideas or variations on those ideas from prior rounds. The process continues with the following rounds until every participant receives their own form returned.

If participants wish to keep their identities private The facilitator could ask them to put all papers in a bowl , and select them each one at a. After that, with a different paper now is the time to examine the concepts and conduct an analysis. Does it look good? How can it be improved? The person who is completing the form should add three additional ideas to the piece of paper they are in possession of. This process is repeated until all boxes of ideas on the form are filled in.

Next step would be to sort these ideas through the group members or by a decision maker. The group members can move the ideas onto post-it notes, group them, before combining and refining the ideas before transferring them to the decision-maker. The last step is to decide on the direction. This can be accomplished by the members of the group or by the executive following the input from the group.

Through the method of brainwriting Participants can build upon one another's ideas, make critiques, and debate different ideas, all while maintaining the illusion of anonymity.

Though brainwriting has numerous advantages It is also one of the brainstorming techniques as well as has its advantages and drawbacks. Brainwriting is the most efficient for the following scenarios:

* Larger groups involved in traditional brainstorming may take a lot of time.

* In working environments where anonymity may make participants more comfortable and relaxed, for instance in politically-charged groups or in groups that have different degrees of leadership.

• In large groups, or during online brainstorming sessions where anonymity is a possibility.

* There is a limited amount of time available to brainstorm ideas.

* The dominant personality of a group might make it difficult for others to speak.

A relatively straightforward topic for brainstorming such as, "How can we answer customers' queries more quickly?" versus "How can we better organize the customer support department?"

* Groups without a certified facilitator who can plan or moderate an informal brainstorming session.

However there are some situations where the likelihood that brain writing can be effective are low. Here are a few examples:

* The group isn't enough For example, less than six persons.

* The brainstorming subject is complex and requires intense and close collaboration among team members.

* The concepts are too complex to be explained in just a few sentences.

* The ideas you're looking for aren't able to be explained in just a few sentences or developed in just a few minutes.

* The members of the group are at ease writing.

Brain walking

Brain walking is a creative exercise similar to the brain writing exercise, however with one major distinction: instead of paper being moved around, participants are moving around. Also instead of handing out idea notes or cards, participants go from station to station and read through the ideas and make remarks or suggestions. Bryan Mattimore, a specialist in facilitation and ideation created brain walking on the concept of brain writing as an extension and built on the same principle of cross-pollinating and building upon the others' ideas. Brain walking was introduced by him in his book of 2012 titled Idea Stormers.

This is how it works after introducing the issue and looking at it from various perspectives, the group selects the most important issues or aspects of the issue as the best spark of inspiration. The facilitator write each prompt down in a huge piece paper, such as A1 flip chart, and then attaches them to a wall. Participants then walk through the "ideation stations." They can add their own ideas or make comments on those already written onto the piece of paper every station.

According to Mattimore, brain walking can be described as the "single most effective way to begin an ideation process" and lists several benefits when compared with other brainstorming methods. In particular, it can increase the enthusiasm in the group as well as fostering a feeling of a shared goal and group identity, providing some privacy while sharing any ideas, looking at the same problem from multiple perspectives, the convenience of leveraging the thoughts of others and ideas, and so on.

Brainwalking can get people out of their chairs, gets the participants moving and keeps their energy levels high. It's an enjoyable and effective technique for creating lots of energy in the group via movement and spark many ideas, without any pitfalls, such as production blockade or evaluation anxiety

Reverse Brainstorming

If you're stuck in the traditional process of brainstorming, it's time to think in your thinking! A most enjoyable and innovative brainstorming methods is known as "reverse brainstorming" sometimes referred to as "negative brainstorming." Reverse brainstorming flips the traditional process of brainstorming upside down. Instead of asking participants to come up with innovative ideas to address a challenge or improve a product you require them to come up with ways to derail the process, making the goal unattainable or even harm the idea or product. Therefore, you let all negative thoughts come to the surface, allowing you to see the things that don't work and the reasons why something could fail. After you've identified the problem, you'll be able to come up with innovative strategies to fix any flaws or deficiencies.

To understand reverse brainstorming better Let's look at it in comparison to conventional brainstorming.

* If a company is looking to come up with strategies to improve its customer service,

the traditional brainstorming might ask "How can we improve our customers' service?". However reverse brainstorming would ask, "How can we make our customer service so bad that our customers aren't using our services and products?"

The traditional brainstorming method asks "How can this project be successful?" while reverse brainstorming attempts to figure out ways to avoid success!

You can employ reverse brainstorming by itself as the primary method of brainstorming or as a complement to regular brainstorming sessions. The combination may be beneficial in the event that regular brainstorming sessions fail to produce satisfactory results because of one or more of the typical mistakes in brainstorming that have been discussed previously or any other reason like the following:

Participants have shared a variety of thoughts and have nothing else to add. However, there isn't a clear direction yet as to how to proceed.

Inviting people to consider ways to make something work is generally simpler than encouraging them to think of new ways to improve it.

* The task isn't easy and the participants are exhausted of it. But, tapping into tension and negative emotions can be a fantastic method to break through that will revive the enthusiasm and energy, and spark creative thinking.

* Participants are so involved in the problem and its specific solutions that they are unable to think of alternative solutions. Reverse brainstorming is an effective method to encourage people to think outside the box.

* The participants have been spent too much time and too quickly on an idea and overlooked other alternatives.

Participants are working to come up with innovative ways to improve the existing product or idea. Reverse brainstorming can help identify the problems and issues. For instance, if would like to enhance your travel application, reverse brainstorming might result in "Try to design an user interface that is extremely complicated to use." This may lead to the conclusion that the app is actually, difficult to navigate for a typical user.

The group is well-versed in the subject and the challenges it presents and is looking to come up with several ideas in the shortest time possible. They understand the negatives as well as what the alternative might be like.

* To connect with people who are currently or will be using the product or idea and to enhance their experience.

The thing that makes reverse brainstorming distinct in the field of brainstorming is the ability to stimulate imagination and positive problem solving by tapping into the negative emotions caused by the issue. Additionally, reverse brainstorming has many other benefits including the following:

* For many discussing problems rather than attempting to find solutions eases anxiety and stress. Reverse brainstorming can leverage this common behavior positively.

It could also begin with a process of exploration when participants start to draw attention to the challenges and issues that would otherwise go by without being noticed.

The typical brainstorming technique tries to think of ways to improve things. However, they may not remove the flaws. Reverse brainstorming can help with this omission of regular brainstorming. That is, you seek out the weaknesses of the product or concept and then figure out how to fix them.

A good illustration of reverse brainstorming is the time when government agencies and corporations employ hackers to penetrate their systems of computers to discover their weaknesses. This "reverse" strategy instead of coming up with the most efficient ways to deter cybercriminals you are trying to emulate the criminals you are targeting and discover the things that aren't working for your security. Reverse brainstorming is a great tool as it will teach you what you should not do.

Therefore, you should try using reverse brainstorming regularly in the beginning, whether as the primary method of brainstorming or after experimenting with other strategies.

Starburst

Starbursting is a map of the questions with six-sided stars that has the main ideation topic in the middle. Each of the six sides is comprised of one of the key words for questions that are: who which, what, where when, why and in what way. It's an easy and effective method of presenting concepts or generating new ones, and making connections between the two.

Starbursting sessions concentrate on the details of the ideas previously gathered. Therefore, it is helpful when conducting the convergent part of brainstorming or in extending the divergent process. It begins with easy clear questions and moves to more intricate and profound ones. The aim is to comprehend and question the assumptions and make sure that every aspect of the chosen concepts have been considered prior to making a decision on the path to take.

It is an equivalent to questions tracking however it there are some distinct differences as well. As opposed to question forming, the star bursting method allows participants to respond to questions right away and then discuss the responses. Furthermore, it's more structured in the form and flow of questions as well as the way in which the participants analyze the responses.

Imagine a company is trying to increase sales. The result of earlier brainstorming sessions involved the creation and launching a mobile application to make shopping more convenient for mobile users. The central question of that star bursting meeting is to figure out how to design and release the mobile application. After writing the question in the center of the star The team then thinks of several questions that are based on each word. Here are a few examples:

• Who are the target users of this application?

• Who is the most common first users?

What are some of our rivals?

* What do we name it?

What are the primary functions of the application?

What are the distinctive advantages of this app?

* Where will we go to create the application?

* Where will we go to announce it?

* Where are the bulk of the customers?

What time do you wish to begin the app?

* When will we begin to promote the app?

* When should we anticipate to see the effect in our revenue?

* Why is it now the best time to start this particular application?

* What is the reason why customers will enjoy this application?

* Why do we believe this app is superior to the other applications?

How can we structure the development team to accomplish our objectives with this application?

* How do we conduct market research to determine the customer's needs and preferences?

* How can we connect our existing services into the new application?

When there are at most three questions in each side of the Star, the group regularly discusses the issues and then writes down a quick answer to each.

Star bursting is a fantastic method to create a focused question to analyze, research, and improve a concept or product. It challenges assumptions and assumptions about the idea. However it is not as effective as a method of brainstorming because it requires an initial idea or subject.

The most significant drawback of Star bursting lies in the fact that it's an unstructured process that can cause it to be difficult to keep the attention and achieve the desired outcome in the timeframe that is reasonable. Therefore, a well-organized facilitation process is essential to manage the participants, the questions and the time.

In the session of starburst for the mobile app that is being developed, John might look at the "Why" area of the star , and inquire "Why should we not employ new staff to create an app rather than burdening the existing staff with greater tasks?" John might have an argument and has made a suggestion that begins by asking "why". But such a query will divert the group from the subject at hand and which will lead them to the treacherous financial waters of HR and finance.

Facilitators play a crucial function in dealing with off-track issues. If they are not addressed, it can derail discussions, while ignoring these could lead to a lack of cooperation. There are two ways to handle such concerns in a safe manner. One option is to prepare an off-topic list of unrelated however important questions and then discuss the issues at a later time. The other alternative is to ask team members to change questions in terms of the discussion the topic. For instance, John's query could be changed to "How do we ensure that our development team finish the project without having to work overtime?"

Star bursting may be affected by common mistakes in brainstorming that were that were discussed within this section including evaluation anxiety as well as dominant personality. So, the facilitator needs to ensure that all participants can contribute their ideas. Standard measures like having a timer in place to deter anyone from trying to "filibuster" the meeting and encouraging everyone to brainstorm questions, addressing off-track issues and so on. These will all aid. In addition, the facilitator might give participants a bit of time to consider their questions before discussing them later. This would be similar to adding writing exercises to the brain-bursting session.

Controlling time is the third problem facing the facilitator of star bursting. The issue of scope creep and production blocking coupled with the flexibility of star bursting could quickly end up destroying the entire session. But, a good facilitation strategy can solve these issues to a large extent. Here are some ways to control the time during the midst of a jam-packed session:

* Allotting only a certain amount of time to each part of the procedure. For instance, 5 minutes to brainstorm what questions you want to ask for every of the corners on the page, 3 minutes to go over each one, etc.

The limit on the amount of questions is set.

* Delegating the debate of the questions for each group to a work group: This may be useful in larger groups of starbursting.

* Brainwalking or using brainwriting to help you answer the questions more quickly.

Role-shaping

This method is designed to help people feel comfortable offering ideas that are completely new. It can help you overcome the fear of being judged by letting team members assume an "role" and then present their ideas in the character. It's similar to the game of role-play, but is utilized to improve the efficiency of organization or any other scenario that requires brainstorming. Role-playing can be a useful and fun method to come up with fresh ideas.

Rolestorming is a distinct type of brainstorming group that involves the role of playing. For instance, participants can take on real-life roles, for example, a client manager, competitor or fictional characters like famous people or superheroes.

The idea behind rolestorming is that engaging in a creative process while playing a part can increase the chance of getting rid of assumptions and thinking in fresh and imaginative ways. It was developed by business expert Rick Griggs in the 1980s the rolestorming method is a collective brainstorming method that takes a fresh look at the most commonly encountered pitfalls in brainstorming. In his time as a leader in several Silicon Valley corporations, Griggs observed that many brainstorming sessions are plagued by the following issues:

The first suggestion is the most effective.

* Evaluation anxiety, i.e. the fear of appearing stupid,

* Following the main personalities,

• Problems with spontaneous thinking.

The primary reason that role-playing can be successful is that it reduces anxiety of the participants. It appears that most people are more comfortable sharing ideas when they are acting in character. Furthermore, they're able to think more creatively since being in character helps them look at the problem from a different perspective and become less focused on the particulars.

The personas of participants significantly affects the effectiveness of role-playing sessions. A demanding or difficult customer or board member historical figures that are connected to the subject of the meeting and famous due to a specific kind of thinking such as a superhero or supervillain, and numerous different personas can be created. Participants could choose to all play the same persona or different ones. They could also pick their own character, or have an assigned character.

It is crucial to keep in mind that rolestorming is more of an exercise than various other brainstorming methods. This is why the process of rolestorming is more focused on having fun and creative acting improvisation. These are some of the examples

* The participants must decide or be aware of their character and should be able to define their character.

Everyone should get lost in their character and refrain from making reference to actual events or limitations, such as the absence of staff or funds.

Participants must be aware that role-playing is more of a game, and that they must be ready and willing to participate. The entire purpose of this kind of brainstorming is to move over the day-to-day challenges, to let the mind go free and look at the issue by exploring angles that would otherwise be unexplored.

Because of the unconventional nature of the process and the role of facilitator is much more crucial as compared to other brainstorming techniques. The person who facilitates a role-stretching session must have acting or improvisation skills and be comfortable with uncertainty or even fun. Additionally, they must be proficient at taking notes in the course of completing, concluding, and creating connections. They should also have a sharp eye for clues and breakthrough ideas. For instance when a person who is a character unhappy customer complains " the lines always jammed!" the facilitator should note that as a possible lead.

A few people are enthralled by role-playing and feel comfortable doing it. However, many find it difficult and embarrassing. It is the responsibility of the facilitator to explain the game's rules to the players and ensure that they feel comfortable and at ease to play.

One of the best ways to begin the process of role-playing is to incorporate about icebreakers or warm-up questions. They can be fun and interactive games that are unrelated to the subject being discussed.

For instance, you could ask them "If our company were an animal which creature would that be? !

It is also crucial to understand how to arrange and implement ideas gathered during the discussion. The facilitator also is a key player. They need to be able use the improvisations and plays and transform them into feasible breakthrough ideas. If needed participants can have another session in which they will examine their ideas and help the facilitator decide on the best way forward.

Braindumping

Most people don't begin an brainstorming session without knowing their preferred methods and ideas. Although it's helpful to know what the issue is prior to starting the brainstorming session taking the time to start the brainstorming session with your mind stuffed with thoughts could be harmful to your thinking process.

Dee Hock, the founder and former chief executive officer for the Visa credit card company, once stated that "The issue is not finding a new and creative ideas in your head rather, how to bring old ideas out." Anyone who is a participant or facilitator of an idea-sharing session must be wary of their own thoughts because we tend to are prone to promoting our pre-determined thoughts, no matter what method of brainstorming is being used. The tendency to stick to our opinions hinders us from being open to the thoughts of others.

Braindumping is a great method to get rid of the disadvantages discussed previously. It's a simple practice that is performed at the start of a brainstorming session in order to enable participants to let go from their pre-determined concepts. By using a braindump exercise each participant writes down their current thoughts as well as any thoughts that come up in their heads about the subject. It is a good idea to "dump" their thoughts in the beginning of the session in order to clear their minds and begin to come up with new and innovative ideas. All ideas are then shared with the group , and briefly discussed , but not critiqued. The facilitator must inform the group that the ideas will be documented and will form an integral part of the final product. When participants are aware that their ideas are secure and secure, they will be more likely to come up with alternative ideas. It's now time to move on to different brainstorming strategies and look for new ideas from a different viewpoint.

It's a fair assumption the beginning of every session must begin with a brainstorm. It is recommended to spend a few minutes prior to the beginning of the meeting to let the participants free from their predetermined thoughts will always increase the likelihood of having a productive brainstorming session.

Brainsteering

This is a more modernized version of the Osborn method. It is based on the same principle however it takes the culture of the company and goals into consideration. In this way it can be an excellent organizational brainstorming instrument.

The concept was first introduced by ex-McKinsey Consultants Kevin as well as

Shawn Coyne in their 2011 book Brainsteering A Better Method to Innovation, brainsteering is a way to take brainstorming as a standard method and "steers" the process more effectively and practical, especially within corporate settings.

The attempts to brainstorm new ideas within corporations are often unsuccessful due to common problems with brainstorming like evaluation anxiety and not focusing on the company's goals and culture as well as the limitations. Instead of merely trying to think of all the possible ideas brainsteering is focused on providing practical and innovative ideas that are within the confines of norms, targets as well as constraints, culture, and targets.

Brainsteering adheres to the principles and rules of conventional brainstorming i.e. that the first emphasis on the number of thoughts, as well as delaying judgements as well as divergent-convergent thought cycles the process of combining and refining ideas etc. What makes brainsteering different is the fact that it puts the whole brainstorming process within the context of a clearly defined box. Instead of presenting an open-ended question that asks participants to think outside the box, the brainsteering process is first a box defined by what the company would like to or will think about, and then it invites participants to think in a creative manner within the confines of that box. When participants are aware of the direction they can channel their energy, the odds of being more productive are increased.

Brainsteering, in essence, is brainstorming, taking actual-world situations into consideration. The people who use brainsteering are not just companies. Non-profit and university organizations and even individuals can benefit from this method. For instance Coyne brothers Coyne brothers have assisted a number of universities in implementing brainsteering for cost reduction initiatives. One example of this was that the objective was to decrease the footprint and cost of computer systems. The school discovered that most students utilize their laptops to browse the internet, do homework, and so on. Therefore, the school was able to provide a subsidy for new laptops for students, and to eliminate all campus computers.

As we have mentioned Brainsteering is based on the fundamental guidelines and principles of traditional brainstorming. But, there are some specific guidelines that can be followed to ensure effective brainsteering sessions. Let's review of the seven golden guidelines to brainsteering:

1. Be aware of your objectives and limits.

If the ideas you've brainstormed exceed what the company can afford to think about the ideas will not be considered all that well. Thinking outside of the box will only be an euphemism if actual circumstances or policies of the company require that you stay within certain box.

Brainsteering begins with understanding the company's objectives and goals, their decision-making process, limitations and limits. These will determine the scope of feasible ideas. For instance, suppose an institution is brainstorming ideas on ways to cut down on operating expenses, and the conclusion would be "update your IT system." But If the top management has already set an IT schedule for coming two years, then the meeting was a wasted time.

This would've proved more productive had the planner for brainstorming collaborated with the top management team to establish an agreed-upon goal that is that was tailored to the needs of the organization and the specific circumstances. For example, good ideas will not require more than the budget of a specific amount and could yield savings or profits within specific areas, in accordance with the general plans for the organization. By defining a clear box, participants in the brainsteering meeting would not spend their time and effort on ideas that need approval from the regulator, large budgets, changes to the organization or any other changes.

The same principle applies to the brainsteering of individuals. If, for instance, you wish to create an additional source of income, but aren't able to do a second job or do overtime work due to the fact that you must look after your family of children. If this is the case, perhaps an online side-job is the best option as you could be able to pursue it during the evenings, on weekends, or at any other time.

2. Ask the correct questions.

The misconception surrounding brainstorming is that it lets the mind run free with the expectation that inspiration and ideas will come along. In reality this method is rarely successful. In order to be successful, brainstorming requires planning and facilitation. And, and most crucially, a clearly defined the question (or inquiries). The ideation session should be centered around a handful of well-defined questions will lead to several of the most effective variations of traditional brainstorming techniques like questionstorming and starbursting.

Good questions are characterized by two traits:

* They force participants to take a fresh approach, which is to force the participants to separate themselves from their old mental models (i.e. how they have was working previously) and view the problem from a fresh view.

* They are precise enough to establish clearly defined boundaries for the ideation space. This helps to guide the ideas more effectively without being overly restricting.

For instance, a consumer product manufacturer who wants to create new products could begin the session by asking questions like "What's the most avoidable issue our customers experience?" or "How does an individual customer utilize our products in a way that isn't expected?"

The amount of questions asked will depend depending on the amount of people in the team and the issue at hand as well as the scope of ideation and so on. There should at least a couple of questions to look at different aspects of the issue.

3. Select the best participants.

Another misconception regarding brainstorming is that having individuals with no background or knowledge regarding the topic of discussion is an effective strategy since they can provide fresh perspectives. But, as we've mentioned earlier in the book about creativity as well as expertise, is specific to a particular area that requires an appropriate amount of knowledge about the subject. In simple terms, in order for a brainsteering meeting to become effective it is crucial to include participants who can respond to the queries. In the case of brainsteering, this is the most fundamental rule to follow that participants must be able to share their firsthand "in deep trenches" understanding of the issue.

Coyne brothers offer a fantastic illustration to illustrate this concept in the book Brainsteering. They describe one of their customers at retail using brainsteering techniques to lower the increasing proportion of delinquency rates. When one of the customers inquired, "What's changed in our operations that might have led to this rise?" a frontline manager said, "Death has become the new bankruptcy!" Upon further discussions it was revealed that some customers who were in debt, were flimsily claiming bankruptcy, or advised their family members to say they're dead, in the hopes that collectors will cease pressing the problem.

A line manager who had particular understanding of the issue gave an opportunity to identify the root of the issue. After some debates the group decided to inform the collection officers to ask firmly, but with sensitivity, for more information when they suspect that a fraud was being played. Untruthful customers will always come out when requested for more details so that the process of collecting could be continued.

4. Set the scene.

Participants in a brainsteering program must be properly orientated prior to the start in the course. The facilitator must clarify the objectives, goals, and the restrictions. They should also be able explain the process of brainsteering and its differences from traditional brainstorming. Brainsteering tends to be slower but it is more thorough than brainstorming. The majority of discussions are held in smaller groups which we'll discuss in the next guideline. It can be helpful to have the facilitator share examples of brainsteering sessions that have been conducted in the past and provides some examples of success to motivate and inspire participants.

5. Create subgroups for discussion of individual issues.

Instead of having a long, continuous conversation with all participants, split the group into subgroups comprising three to five members and ask them to lead numerous, focused sessions of ideation. The smaller subgroups are more likely to encourage participants to speak out, while the usual practice in larger groups is to remain silent. Set a few questions for each subgroup , and request them to discuss the issues for a predetermined time frame, like one hour.

The proper facilitation of subgroups is vital, particularly dealing with participants who hinder others from sharing their thoughts such as individuals with higher levels of organizational rank (the bosses) and those with large mouths. Facilitators are also able to instruct the subgroups on how to utilize methods like braindumping or reverse brainstorming.

Certain of the principles mentioned above are not applicable to the individual brainsteering. When you're trying to come up with innovative solutions to address a challenge within your budget and potential There aren't any subgroups, and most likely you're thinking for yourself. The most important thing is to focus on the basic principles of brainsteering. You must have a clear understanding of your goals, potential and limits and attempt to think within the boundaries. You are always able to seek advice from people around you. In this case you'll be an active participant as well as the facilitator in the process of ideation.

6. End the session.

After all discussions in the subgroups have concluded, the most ineffective idea is to allow the whole group to pick their preferred ideas from the stack. There are two reasons to this:

* The participants may not have an executive level understanding of priority issues and the criteria for making decisions to pick the most effective options.

* Making a decision on a winning strategy before the group can be demotivating for many of the participants. It might even be unimportant when the actual decision-makers decide to overrule the decision-making group's brainsteering.

An alternative is to have each group focus on their ideas and pick their favorite ideas before sharing ideas with the entire group, with a note about how to proceed and the time to anticipate the best suggestions.

7. Make contact as quickly as you can.

Brainsteering sessions require two follow-ups. The first one involves the management at the top for making decisions, while the second is for participants to discuss the results.

The follow-up with management must be prompt and swift. The top management should evaluate the concepts for immediate implementation, instant rejection, or implementation when it is most convenient or for further reviews. The facilitator or the manager will inform participants about the choices made and the motives.

Stepladder Brainstorming

Like the name suggests, this is a process that is step-by-step to build an "ladder" of ideas that can be used to tackle a dilemma or to make the decision. The most significant benefit of this method is that it inspires all participants regardless of whether they tend to shy and are shy. It begins by explaining the problem to all members of the group. After everyone is aware of the issue then everyone should leave the room with only two persons. Then, let those two individuals work together to brainstorm ideas. When they're done, add one person to the room. The person added will speak about his thoughts prior to the two previous members share their thoughts. Then, let another enter the room and repeat the process until all team members are together in the room. After everyone has discussed their ideas and all participants are in the room, you are able to begin the discussion to make the final decision.

The stepladder method was originally designed as a tool for making decisions. The idea of the technique is that in any team there are certain members who have a tendency to express their views. In order to get everyone's opinion, it's crucial to allow everyone the opportunity to express their opinions. That's the reason, as we talked about prior to this section prominent personalities could impede brainstorming sessions. Thus, the stepladder might be a great way to brainstorm when there are two or three team members who have a more vocal personality than the others , or if some members remain in the group.

Charrette Procedure

The Charrette procedure was designed to aid a huge group of people discuss some or all of the issues. The name is derived directly from the French word "charrette," meaning "cart."In the 19th century, carts were used to transport and collect sketches of architecture students to mark. The Charrette process is the same similar thing.

In the beginning, participants are separated into smaller groups at most five participants. Then, the subgroups begin to discuss the problem at the same time. Ideas from each group is passed over to the following group to discuss and improvement. Then all ideas are collated then discussed, prioritized and ranked. If there are many discussions topics, each group will begin with a single topic. Then, the topics and ideas will move between groups.

The Charrette method is a great way to brainstorm ideas in the following situations:

* There is a significant amount in participants (e.g. more than fifteen).

There are a variety of discussions issues

* The time available is limited, or organizers want to restrict the time for discussion in a deliberate way.

We would love all participants to be part of the discussion.

The Charrette process can produce excellent results since each subgroup polishes and refines most well-known ideas.

Brainstorming online (aka Brain-netting)

We've already talked about ideas generation in face-to face groups. What happens when participants are remote, working across different countries, or in multiple time zones? This is the reason online brainstorming comes to the rescue!

Online brainstorming is an online brainstorming session that is computer-mediated. With the advancement of tools and software online brainstorming, it is more efficient now than before. In addition, due to the current virtual working model, remote meetings are becoming the norm and, sometimes, the only alternative in many companies. Therefore, it's important to talk about online brainstorming and the tools it uses more in depth.

Online brainstorming isn't an original method, like brainsteering or rolestorming. It's more about implementing the current methods efficiently and efficiently using a broad variety technology. Today, nearly everyone utilizes chat apps, group calls and video-conferencing as the principal methods to communicate on the internet (apart from sending emails to each other!). But what happens if the group members are looking to collaborate on whiteboards or documents, engage in through a face-to-face meeting, or participate in tasks such as mind-mapping? An easy and affordable alternative to let members of your team to collaborate online is to make use of collaborative documents, such as Google Docs that allow several users to edit, write and highlight an Excel spreadsheet or document and make comments. However, if you want to chat while editing, you'll have to integrate Google Docs with a conferencing system such as Skype.

The next stage is all-in-one business suites that let team members communicate with each other, share screens, access shared folders, hold video conferences, and more. The most popular choices comprise Skype for Business, WebEx as well as Microsoft Teams.

In the case of the process of brainstorming online, tools can be invaluable, particularly in the event that all or some of the participants work remotely. There are a myriad of applications that offer different capabilities and pricing ranges that can aid both you and the team to participate in online brainstorming. Online tools have been designed to allow collaborative digital brainstorming and provide features that are not found in traditional business suites.

There are two types of online tools for brainstorming Mind mapping tools online as well as virtual boards. Here are a few examples from each category:

Online mind mapping tools for the brain

1. Bubbl.us The platform on the web provides mind maps and lets you build an idea tree by beginning with a basic idea, and adding more ideas on different levels. There is no need to download any application as everything is hosted on the internet. Bubble.us offers three plans. Basic functions are available for free, however you can purchase the paid version after the 30 day trial period for a free upgrade to more features.

2. Freeplane: Freeplane enables users to create and connect subtopics and topics and also add shapes, colors and images as required. It can also help you categorize, place and arrange various factors relevant to the issue. Additionally, it's extremely user-friendly as it allows you to drag and drop objects on the screen.

3. Popplet: Popplet is a excellent choice for those trying to inspire students to brainstorm as a part of a school activity. It can also be used in workplace scenarios

because it allows multiple users to access simultaneously. Furthermore, you can create presentations using visualizations and diagrams. It was developed for Android however, it's available to iOS users.

4. MindMap is available through Google Chrome's extension, MindMap is a great tool for brainstorming. It comes featuring Google Drive, Dropbox, and Cloud all included to the service's support. With this program, you can sketch an image with your fingers and add them to the mindmap.

5. FreeMind: To brainstorm with your friends FreeMind is a great alternative. It can be used with Windows, Linux, or Mac computers. It features a one-click navigation panel that lets you upload images, drag-and-drop and even import previously created mindmaps.

6. Coggle: This program allows users build interactive brain maps that take the form of complex visual networks. Members of the team have access to a shared mini map and brainstorm ideas for the central

idea in real time and then incorporate it into your mindmap. The map contains multiple branches that are displayed in various shades. Each branch is a collection of ideas that are related.

7. MindMeister MindMeister: It's an extremely powerful online mind mapping tool that includes collaboration capabilities, such as an integrated chat function , and the ability to comment and vote on concepts. The service is completely free and allows users to create three mind maps. The paid version is extremely affordable at just $ 4.99 each month, for unlimited maps.

Virtual boards

1. IdeaBoardz It is a no-cost web-based virtual board that allows collaborators to create their own ideas with sticky notes that are virtual, arrange ideas in various sections, cast votes for their top ideas, then sort ideas according to the highest number of sections or votes, search for keywords, and then export the boards for future discussions.

IdeaBoardz offers the digital equivalent of whiteboard or flip chart and can be utilized in a variety of brainstorming techniques, including online brainwriting , reverse brainstorming or even reverse brainstorming.

2. Realtime Board: It's an online whiteboard for collaboration space, complete with virtual post-it-notes. Along with putting their ideas to sticky notes, participants can upload images, files, and documents. When the meeting is over the notes and other files can be converted into a slide presentation or PDF file. Realtime Board has both free and paid versions.

3. MURAL: This online visual collaboration tool provides the virtual Board, powerful facilitation functions like timers and voting and a canvas for adding notes and shapes.

Tools like those mentioned above are crucial for conducting an online session of brainstorming. Like any other method of brainstorming the proper preparation as well as facilitation for the session is vital. Additionally, online brainstorming presents its own unique issues. For instance, working with groups of people across time and space brings up fundamental problems that are not present in face-to-face brainstorming. To facilitate online brainstorming to be a successful process, both the facilitator and the participants need to be aware of particular issues and implement strategies to deal with these issues. Let's go over some of these issues , and then the guidelines to reduce their impact

Team members who are who are in different time zones can create serious scheduling issues. For one thing finding the best time to include individuals in Singapore, London, and San Fransico in the same online meeting isn't an easy task. In many instances there are at least a few parts of the online brainstorming need to occur synchronously. We'll go over this in the near future.

* Not all are technologically proficient. Some participants may not be able use the online brainstorming tools effectively or to resolve IT problems.

* If some of the participants have Mac computers, and other PCs, there could be certain compatibility issues.

Effective using online tool for online brainstorming requires time and effort. The initial few sessions can be unproductive and messy because participants are learning.

* If the team comprises freelancers or contractors They may do not access the network internal or the paid version the tools for brainstorming.

There is a way to address each of these problems quickly, with the exception of the first one. The majority of people learn to utilize mental maps and virtual boards to overcome IT problems. However, collaborating across time zones is more difficult to solve. However sophisticated the tools may be, eventually brainstorming requires the cooperation of humans. What can a group do to work in a group if certain members are asleep while others are at the middle or at the end their working day?

The best solution is to divide your brainstorming into synchronous and asynchronous elements. Video or audio chats online are "synchronous" instances of collaboration. This means that they require all participants to be in sync unlike "asynchronous" instances in the brainstorming process. These is that people can finish a portion of the process independently.

The best strategy is to communicate the question you want to ask, along with some context, objectives, and limitations, to participants via email or by sharing a document like an Google Doc and ask the group to consider the issue at whatever time is suitable for each member of the team. By doing this you make use of the synchronous portion of brainstorming to generate ideas. Team members then can communicate their ideas to the facilitator, or directly upload them to your virtual boards or virtual mind maps online.

The next step is to bring all of the team on an audio or video chat to discuss ideas and consider the subject in different ways. It is

154

called the synchronous aspect of the process. This is where you talk about, discuss and mix ideas.

This asynchronous-synchronous cycle can happen several times until reaching the desired outcome. For instance, following the initial call, participants may spend some time thinking about the thoughts and ideas they heard during the call and add their own ideas to the boards or itineraries, or even sort and blend the ones they already have. They can then join a subsequent call with their comments.

We discussed interactive brainwriting during this section. We also discussed how people can communicate their ideas and engage both synchronously and asynchronously. The ability to take time to consider suggested ideas could result in more thoughtful brainstorming. In that way online brainstorming can provide the advantages of writing.

Similar to traditional brainstorming, requires skilled facilitation and an understanding of the issue, process participants, goals and limitations.

Additionally, the facilitators of an online brainstorming session must pick the appropriate methods and tools, and then manage the synchronous collaboration. Other brainstorming methods, like braindumping, can be included in online brainstorming. Also, don't forget keep in touch with participants about the results and lessons learned from the brainstorming session.

We have covered a variety of brainstorming strategies within this chapter. The next two chapters will explore the application of these techniques for groups and in personal and professional contexts. Effective brainstorming may feel like an achievement for all involved because it feels like the process was worthwhile and worth the effort and time. How do you decide between these tools and use them to come up with innovative ideas for your business or in your personal life? The answer will be revealed in the coming chapters!

Chapter 7: Brainstorming With Groups

Group brainstorming is at the basis of collaborative ideas in many professional settings around the globe. If it is done properly it can foster creativity, boost the spirit of the team and aid the team find breakthrough ideas. We've discussed the fundamentals of brainstorming as well as related methods in earlier chapters. This chapter will discuss how to run a successful group brainstorming session whether face-to-face or via online. We will also discuss effective facilitation and brainstorming mistakes to avoid, and ways to use the online tool to facilitate better brainstorming.

Is Group Brainstorming Still Relevant?

Before we get into the intricacies of brainstorming in groups, let's be a bit more cautious and look at whether brainstorming in groups is still logical. If you inform a coworker at work that the next meeting will be an open-ended brainstorming session it is likely that you'll receive eyes rolling and groans. Many people believe that brainstorming is logical, but doesn't perform in actual practice. Many think that brainstorming is as outdated and unnecessary waste of time. What is the reason why brainstorming is still used in the business world? Does it remain a valid and useful idea?

We'll leave the discussion of the differences between individuals and groups brainstorming until the next chapter, and then concentrate on the reason the reason why group brainstorming is been criticized by certain people. Many critics of brainstorming and those who have had negative experiences in brainstorming tend to tend to think of traditional brainstorming and not the more contemporary variations which we discussed in the preceding chapter. Here are a few of the most frequent concerns about brainstorming in groups:

The act of expressing ideas in a setting with others is not for everyone for instance, due to the fear of being considered a failure.

* Not all people are good in the rapid generation of ideas.

* It is too long.

* Not everyone is part of the process of thinking.

* A group of people can become obsessed with a specific concept.

* You must wait for other people to arrive.

* You come with clear-cut thoughts.

* Participants tend to prefer more traditional opinions.

* Introverts are less likely express their thoughts in a public forum.

* One person speaks while the others listen, not think of their own thoughts.

We explored the various complaints that we have as the drawbacks from traditional brainstorming techniques in our previous chapter. Additionally, we learned that the latest brainstorming methods can solve every one of the traditional disadvantages of brainstorming while still benefiting from the synergy effect of a group. Brainwriting, for instance, allows introverts to express their thoughts without having to speak within the group and braindumping can take the obvious ideas out of the equation. Similar to the stepladder, Charrette allows everyone to be involved in the process of thinking, and brainsteering can be a useful method for effective brainstorming in both professional and personal settings.

The benefits that can be derived from group brainstorming can be enormous. The most important benefit is the synergy that occurs within the group, i.e., taking advantage of the group's collective knowledge and power of mind. Synergy between groups allows participants to come up with something greater than the totality of their components. If one person is struggling with an idea, a different member can draw on their imagination and experience to elevate the idea to the next step. The group members can offer feedback, improve upon the ideas of others and then mix and improve their ideas. In addition, successful brainstorming with a group encourages group ownership of the concepts because everyone participates in creating the ideas.

However, does group brainstorming be effective? Not necessarily. It is it possible to hold an effective brainstorming group? Absolutely! The process of group brainstorming is similar to performing an DIY project. If you've got the abilities, utilize the appropriate tools, and plan and budget your project well and you will be able to get your DIY project completed in acceptable quality and save lots of cost.

In the same way, effective brainstorming requires appropriate tools as well as strategies as well as proper planning and execution. It is equally true that saying that "Brainstorming isn't effective!" or "Brainstorming is obsolete and wastes the time!" is as valid and pertinent as the statement "DIY projects don't work!" Sure, many people have regrets about their DIY ventures. Yet, many other people have plans and complete a variety of DIY projects with skill. The real solution to "Does the group-thinking process work?" is "It depends!"

The effectiveness of group brainstorming is due to two primary elements:

1. Selecting the best brainstorming method.

2. Proper setup and execution prior to, during, and following the session.

What are the most important actions should you as a participant organizer, or facilitator, follow to get the most of the group brainstorming sessions? What are the best practices and don'ts of effective group brainstorming?

Chapter 4 covered brainstorming tools and methods in greater detail. There's always a good techniquefor face-to face or via the internet, for an intimate or large group or for brainstorming in a group or on your own. It is always possible to revisit Chapter 4 and choose the method that suits your situation the most. As you will see, I'm not talking about Chapter 2. That is to say I would not suggest using the classic Osborn-style brainstorming to avoid common mistakes at all.

This chapter will discuss the second aspect that is crucial to successful gathering brainstorming in groups. i.e. how to plan the setting up, planning, and execution, with a particular focus on the effective facilitation and management of group's dynamics. We begin by setting the scene to facilitate the session. We will proceed through each phase of the process step-by-step.

You might be part of the discussion in all meetings for brainstorming however, you could also be the facilitator or organizer at times. The best method to master the specifics involved in the procedure is to envision you are the facilitator for the planned session. The facilitator is in charge of the preparation and setting up of the session. He is aware of the group's personality and dynamics, and actively guides the discussion and is able to alter the direction. Understanding the fundamentals and procedures of a productive brainstorming session can help participants. The optimal scenario is that participants are as well-versed about how to conduct the session as is the facilitator. Therefore, for the remainder part of the chapter you're the facilitator and participant in an imaginary brainstorming session hoping to create the most awesome brainstorming session ever!

Ten Guaranteed Ways to End an Brainstorming Session

Let's have an exercise in negative brainstorming! What can you do to avoid having terrible brainstorming sessions? One which frustrates and demotivates all participants, organizers facilitators, managers and so on.? What is what you should be avoiding during your brainstorming session.

According to my experiences there are ten key traits of a boring and unproductive brainstorm . It eats away time and energy is a source of frustration for everyone and produces zero results. If you can stay clear of these ten mistakes then you'll be ahead of the majority of brainstormers.

1. This is a way of destroying the purpose behind brainstorming

Let's get started with the fundamentals. The entire purpose behind thinking about brainstorming and brainstorming is to let the creativity come out and shine. If you're looking to ensure that your brainstorming session is not productive you must thwart your creativity! There are many methods to achieve this. For instance, you could practice saying this anywhere in the room:

* "Everyone get started tossing around ideas!"

* "We must get away from this place with a brilliant idea!"

* "Don't be a waste of time and energy with absurdity!"

* "Let me start the session by sharing my thoughts!"

* "We've done it before!"

* "Everybody Please remain at your table!"

Each of these statements indicates an unsound mindset and lack of facilitation , which can undermine the entire event.

A request for action like "Start with a brainstorm!" inspires nobody. Thinking creatively or solving problems is an act. It takes time to develop and is accomplished through divergent and convergent thought cycles. It is a terrible method of encouraging creativity. In the end, the usual suspects dominate the group while the others are doodles or just daydreaming.

What happens if the meeting generates more than one great idea? Perhaps there isn't a clear breakthrough idea? A predetermined goal hinders creativity as the participants are focused on pleasing the facilitator or organizer. Instead the emphasis should be on getting the participants involved, creating an enjoyable flow of ideas as well as making positive and positive group dynamic.

In many instances, the participants in the group brainstorming sessions aren't in fact the primary decision makers to select the most effective idea. A successful brainstorming session includes an adequately defined problem statement as well as specific goals and limitations. However, this doesn't mean that you should set strict goals. If the meeting is planned well and executed well, there's often plenty of great ideas.

The phrases "Let's go out with a great concept!" and "Don't waste our time with silly ideas!" usually go hand with each other. When the facilitator or participant in a brainstorming session says these phrases they're determined to reduce time and effort and will be able to provide a lot of boring ideas! What is the best way to tell if the idea isn't real? If it doesn't seem to make sense on first sight Is it really untrue? It's not unusual to realize that some ideas are not feasible or even beneficial. But to discard them fast and fast is not in line with the very purpose of brainstorming.

Brainstorming should be a secure space for thinking creatively as well as exploring new ideas and trying out new concepts. It should let the mind be free and fun and not labeling every concept in the brainstorming session as "nonsense." Every new ideas may seem absurd initially. One of the most dangerous actions you can take during brainstorming sessions is to deny "nonsense"! However facilitators and their organizers should encourage the sharing of insane and bizarre ideas. Perhaps they are crazy or ineffective. However, they could be the foundation for rational and enthralling concepts.

Requiring people to sit down or even suggesting that is a mistake that is often made. The movement of people creates energy that leads to more and better ideas. The brainstorming session must be in a an informal and relaxed environment to ease anxiety and let the mind be free. It is acceptable to speak when walking or standing. Actually, many brainstorming methods, such as the stepladder, brainwalking, or collaborative brainwriting, heavily depend on the creation of movement within the group.

We then come to the most dangerous statement: "We've tried it before!" and its many variations like "We don't think we should do things this method" as well as "The world isn't working that in that way!" etc. These statements are like shooting an idea with a shotgun , and are completely counterproductive to innovative thinking. The goal is to be wary of these messages during the divergent stage of brainstorming. Of course, analysis and editing are vital components of brainstorming that work. But only after all ideas have been gathered, it's time to move on to the convergence phase.

Ideas are fragile , and erroneous phrases can bring the entire session to a standstill. If you're looking to enjoy an interesting and stimulating brainstorming session, avoid the kinds of statements like those previously mentioned.

2. Being ill-prepared

A poorly planned and executed brainstorming sessions are little more than wasted effort, unhappy participants, and a pile of unfinished ideas.

Planning a brainstorming session involves a variety of aspects and making decisions on various elements. Here are some of the most common scenarios:

The basic elements of the meeting including how many people are in the room, duration of the meeting, the participants, etc.

* Technique for brainstorming along with Format (in person or via virtual)

* Communication with stakeholder

• Selecting a competent Facilitator (in instance you're an one who organizes)

Perhaps the brainstorming session will last just 30 minutes. But the process should be well-organized before the group gets together. The person in charge of the group should define the topic and the context and limitations. Once the fundamentals of the session's scope and purpose are established the facilitator will be able to create a set of questions that will ensure that the group is headed in the right direction.

When we talk about preparation and preparation, we're also talking about arming the participants before hand, providing them with the necessary information ahead of the meeting. After that, you can have them think of their ideas, and use the time to discuss and share them.

The advantage of discussing the topic of discussion and the background information in advance is that it allows the ideas to settle within their heads, creating an incubation time. This will help to spark new ideas in the course of the meeting. Plus, the first knowledge of the problem will mean that you won't need to be wasting time explaining the problem.

All of these steps take time and energy , and is not what most people consider brainstorming. The most popular myth is that brainstorming involves cobbling meetings at very short notice, inviting only several people and then attending the meeting with no preparation. People believe that brainstorming is an unplanned process and is best done in the midst of things. Some even believe that preparation and facilitation might stop the flow of ideas.

The notion that you must to break free of the framework to be innovative is a fundamental misinterpretation of the process of brainstorming particularly group brainstorming. Similar to any other group activity planning, preparation and guidance are crucial to successful brainstorming. The ability to let loose of the structure can be beneficial during the process of brainstorming that is divergent, However, it is not the beginning or the final phases. We will go over the steps involved in preparing in more depth later in this chapter.

3. The answer is unclear or incorrect

Sometimes, the participants engage in a brainstorming session only to discover that they did not address the issue at hand because the statement of problem was inaccurate, in error or not properly phrased. A similar problem that is rephrased in various forms could have various solutions. As an example, let's say you (or your company) are having a difficult time dealing with the demands of the job. In search of ideas on how to manage the situation it is possible to ask yourself, "How can I finish all my tasks before the month's end?" The possible answers include working more hours or working during the weekend and working more efficiently and so on. However, imagine replacing this question "How do I finish all my work completed before the month is over?" This question approaches the problem from a different angle and leads to suggestions for involving others to complete the work.

Perhaps a real-world scenario will help to make the point more clear. In 1955, the first commercial television began broadcasting throughout The UK. Broadcasting rights auctioned off in 1954. Several parties trying to figure out which region would generate the highest amount of advertising revenues. The majority of analysts believed that the wealthiest regions would be the top spending regions. Therefore, they asked, "How do we get broadcasting rights for the most prosperous areas?" But One man took a different view. Sidney Bernstein from Granada Television claimed that, instead of bidding on the richest regions, it is better to focus on the most watched regions. Then, he thought, "How do I get broadcasting rights in the areas where people are most likely to watch TV?" His different take on the issue resulted in him bidding on the most slushy regions in which the majority of people are watching television! This led to Granada Television eventually got broadcasting rights in the north of the rainy region in the UK and eventually became one of the most profitable British production companies for TV.

When trying to formulate a problem-solving questions, it's generally easier to concentrate on the symptoms instead of the root of the issue. One approach for avoiding this problem is asking multiple why-questions in order to identify the root of the issue. Here's an illustration. Let's say you wish to increase the time-to-finish of projects you manage. If you ask "How do we complete the tasks in time?" it will be too broad and vague to address. Therefore, it is better to begin by asking some questions to discover the true source of the problem. For example:

The projects aren't completed in time. Why?

* They're not starting in time. Why?

* The department charged with the task is overloaded. Why?
* Due to the fact that they're not adequately staffed.

The questions continue until the issue is obvious enough. This may seem simple, however asking "why" can lead you to delve deeper into every circumstance. To answer an "why" question it is essential to be aware of what's going on in the setting. We'll go over how to create innovative and interesting problems statements more in depth later on in this chapter.

4. Uncertain constraints and expectations

The challenge of brainstorming effectively without knowing the limitations and expectations is just like winning a soccer match without knowing the location of the goalposts and how far from one another.

This erroneous belief is inextricably linked to thinking that there is no structure or creating plans to spur creativity. Many people are unable to grasp the importance of thinking outside-of-the-box when brainstorming. There are always limits to what is possible and practical in terms of money, time and regulations. This is true for both businesses and individuals.

The previous chapter dealt with brainsteering as a variation of traditional brainstorming that considers context, goals, and constraints into consideration. The constraints may include not exceeding a particular budget, or limiting the available time, or having specific objectives. These constraints determine the range of feasible solutions. This may seem counterintuitive to some. On one the other hand, brainstorming involves creative and innovative thinking. However it is essential to have an organized set of goals and limitations. What can we do to find a way to reconcile these two?

The most important thing is to understand that brainstorming goes beyond the divergent stage that is commonly referred to by a lot of people. It is so typical that many people view brainstorming as attending an event, discussing some thoughts about the subject and then leaving, believing that their ideas will magically solve the issue.

A productive brainstorming session is comprised of several stages, both convergent and divergent that each have their own unique method of thinking and strategy. It is important to note that brainstorming can also involve mixing, refining and the clustering of ideas. Therefore, while the original idea could be rejected by the limits you set however, it can be refined to meet criteria.

5. Insufficient orientation

Are you aware of being dragged away from work to attend a conference and you were then required to think outside of the box and come up with new ideas? Without a proper understanding of the situation, the context, boundary conditions the brainstorming method, and the process, people are unable to comprehend the situation and what they can expect from the discussion. They are more likely to make up uninformed opinions or adopt a rigid viewpoint, and remain in a good standing with the group.

An appropriate orientation sets the stage and tone for the session and helps the group in getting to the final goal. The process of orienting the participants should begin before the session starts by giving all of the information necessary to understand the issue and the planned session. When the session is set to begin the facilitator needs to clarify the issue and present the brainstorming method.

Furthermore, establishing the rules of brainstorming is a crucial element of the entire process. One of the most crucial rules is the one that bans criticisms during the divergent thinking phase. The most important thing is for one team member to begin bursting out criticisms that slow down any flow to the discussion. This is the reason why facilitators must convince group members that criticisms should be reserved for the later phases of the discussion after you've gotten past divergent thinking to begin with the convergent approach. Facilitators must always be on the lookout for any indications such as a peep or a mumble that could impede the outcomes during the divergent part. At this point the facilitator acts similar to a referee, who ensures that everyone on the field is within the imaginary boundaries set in the rules of play.

6. Not Having Everyone Contribute

The entire purpose behind brainstorming in groups is to harness the collective power of all members and in order to do thateveryone has the opportunity to participate.

The problem could be more serious than just those who are not speaking. That is the output of brainstorming is not just affected by people who are more introverted, and unable to contribute, but also due to fewer individual contributions.

Beyond the individual personalities, the group dynamics and psychological influences play an important impact on how successful group brainstorming will be. Numerous studies have shown that individual brainstorming can produce more ideas than brainstorming in groups. We will explore this contradictory discovery in greater detail in the following chapter. The main reason for this is that the dynamic of the group can be a bit sour. In fact, some of the most knowledgeable and skilled people in the team may perform poorly, because of two psychological influences:

* Social Matching: It refers to the tendency of participants to be matched with the lowest productivity level that is seen within the group. This is similar to the regression to the mean in which a handful of snarky and unmotivated members can bring down the entire team down.

* Social Loafing occurs the case when people are less productive in a social setting than they would on their own. People tend to be more inclined to social loafing when they believe that their individual efforts don't make a difference to the group, or they don't get enough respect.

The result of these mental effects are that better-equipped members of the group tone their contribution down. One reason is that brainstorming participants recognize that there are a lot of freeloaders. This is the case, for instance, when the team leader or person who is organizing the session is able to take the ideas and present the ideas to administration as their personal.

The session's planning, correct orientation and facilitation, using methods that allow for greater anonymity such as brainwriting can to improve the dynamics of the group. Other elements like corporate culture and management also play a role however they are more difficult to change.

7. The search for ideas is too short too quickly

Brainstorming is a structured method of thinking that is productive and a deliberate attempt to generate as many ideas as you can and get them to sexual relations with each other and, hopefully, come up with better and more innovative ideas. If we consider brainstorming as an Darwinian process of evolution and selection the variety and quantity of ideas are essential for brainstorming sessions to succeed. The more ideas, the greater chance that some of them will survive.

The inability to stop the divergent thinking process of brainstorming can be an effective way to stop the brainstorming session. You might be wondering how to tell when the brainstorming should continue. If the group members quickly agree on a concept and attempt to argue that it's the most effective feasible idea, or stick to those that are obvious The group must continue considering.

The author of the book Think Better, Tim Hurson discusses how in the initial third ideas are typically the most obvious ones during the course of an ideation. The second third begins to get more creative, but it is generally subpar. It's in the third third of ideas that our brains begin to develop creativity since we've exhausted all the obvious and semi-obvious concepts. Staying with the obvious options suggests that the team remains in the first third, or perhaps within the third quarter of possibilities. Of course, nobody can be sure that the divergent stage will result with a breakthrough concept. In the same way that the more diverse ecosystem has a greater chance of one or two surviving an extensive array of ideas increases the chances of some being a breakthrough.

8. A facilitator who is not trained

In the end, it will be evident how important it is to hire a qualified facilitator who can lead the group brainstorming sessions. If you don't have a qualified facilitator who understands everything discussed in this book and is aware of the role that brainstorming plays as a creative process for problem solving to run an effective brainstorming session will be only shooting in the dark.

One of the most costly mistakes an organization could make in facilitation is letting the boss act as facilitator. In such a session the participants will be self-censoring and the facilitator will alter the content according to what they believe is the best way to do it. In addition, managers are typically so busy in the day-today management of the company that they aren't able to properly plan the meeting and monitor immediately afterward.

Conclusion

Congrats on finishing the book! I hope that you've enjoyed it so far and gained useful new ideas on creativity and brainstorming. It's time to revisit the main points of each chapter, and the main conclusions from the book.

We began our journey by asking the fundamental question: How do you come up with new ideas for creative problem solving? Although the result of a creative process is not certain however, the way to these results is illuminated by a variety of lamp posts. This book sought to determine the lamp posts that can help you find inventive solutions for your little or big issues.